A BRIDGE TO DIALOGUE

Studies in Judaism and Christianity

Exploration of Issues in the Contemporary Dialogue Between Christians and Jews

Editor in Chief for
Stimulus Books
Helga Croner

Editors
Lawrence Boadt, C.S.P.
Helga Croner
Leon Klenicki
John Koenig
Kevin A. Lynch, C.S.P.

 A STIMULUS BOOK

A BRIDGE TO DIALOGUE

The Story of Jewish-Christian Relations

by
John Rousmaniere

Edited by
James A. Carpenter
and Leon Klenicki

**Sponsored by Ecumenical Office of the Episcopal Church
and the Anti-Defamation League of B'nai B'rith**

A STIMULUS BOOK
PAULIST PRESS ♦ NEW YORK ♦ MAHWAH

Library of Congress Cataloging-in-Publication Data

Rousmaniere, John, 1944–
    A bridge to dialogue: the story of Jewish-Christian relations/by John Rousmaniere; edited by James A. Carpenter and Leon Klenicki.
        p. cm.—(A Stimulus book)
    Includes bibliographical references and index.
    ISBN 0-8091-3284-2
    1. Judaism—Relations—Christianity—History. 2. Christianity and other religions —Judaism—History. 3. Christianity and antisemitism—History. 4. Judaism (Christian theology)—History of doctrines. I. Carpenter, James A., 1958–   . II. Klenicki, Leon. III. Title.
    BM535.R647 1991
    261.2′6′09—dc20   91-30794
                                                                        CIP

Published by Paulist Press
997 Macarthur Boulevard
Mahwah, N.J. 07430

Printed and bound in the United States of America

Contents

Introduction
by James A. Carpenter, Leon Klenicki 1

Preface
by John Rousmaniere 3

I. Jews and Christians in the First Century 5

II. Rabbinic Judaism and Early Christianity:
Confrontation and Rivalry 24

III. The Heritage of Hate 42

IV. Further Stages of Conflict in Europe 56

V. Jews in America and the Challenge of Religious Pluralism ... 80

VI. The Twentieth Century: A Time of Extremes 106

Appendices

I. Jewish Foundations of Christian Worship 127

II. Some Recent Christian Documents and Guidelines on Jews
and Judaism 145

Index 146

Introduction

Reverend James A. Carpenter *and Rabbi Leon Klenicki*

The author of this work describes in vivid detail the history of Jewish-Christian relations, from the first century until the present. It is not a pretty history; it is full of misunderstanding and hatred, bigotry and violence. It is a part of history that has little place in standard historical accounts of Christianity, and virtually no place in Christian catechesis, whether in seminaries or parish churches, at least until lately. Christians have been and still are almost totally uninformed about aspects of Christian history that have had dire consequences for the Jews and brought down upon them immense suffering. Christians need to hear the story from the beginning to grasp its impact on Christian consciousness and actions through the centuries. The editors of this book believe that the author has outlined the story well, and that his outline can be of service to the Christian community at a number of levels, principally in furthering relations between Christians and Jews, by providing grist for dialogue between them and showing how important and urgent that dialogue is for the future.

Though this book is jointly sponsored by the Ecumenical Office of the Episcopal Church and the Anti-Defamation League and jointly edited by a Christian and a Jew, the story is written by a Christian author primarily for Christians. It is a story, however, that Jews would like Christians to hear. The venture, therefore, is a cooperative one, marking a great deal of mutual questioning, common discussion and dialogue among all involved, before its appearance in print.

The treatment of material is not exhaustive; not everything can be included in one volume. Much more can and should be said about all the issues raised. There are, no doubt, slanted views presented in the book as

1

well. A number of issues may require more balance, and either more temperate expression on the one hand or a more vehement one on the other. We believe, however, that the work is accurate and that it gathers into brief compass the main forms and forces, historical, theological and political, that have governed Christian attitudes and actions toward the Jews, and that it throws light upon them more than enough to warrant its publication.

We hope that the volume will make its way into the libraries of seminaries and parish churches, and, above all, that it will be used in church-school instructions, adult discussion groups and as a basis for increasing and deepening dialogue between Christian churches and synagogues at the local level. As the title suggests, the book is to serve as a means for Christian self-discovery and encounter with Jewish history and Jewish life today.

There are two appendices, one with a list of various documents on Jewish-Christian relations and one on Christian indebtedness to Jewish sources for many of its specific liturgical forms and its general patterns of worship. This appendix might serve as an additional focus for discussion and dialogue.

The editors are grateful to the Anti-Defamation League and the Ecumenical Office of the Episcopal Church for sponsoring the project, to the Committee on Christian-Jewish relations advisory to the Presiding Bishop of the Episcopal Church for editorial advice and encouragement, and to William Stokes, student assistant to Dr. Carpenter, for editorial work of a high order.

Preface

John Rousmaniere

The story of how Christians and Jews have lived with and, more often, against each other is a painful one, but it is a story that Christians should know. Knowledge is the bridge to the intimate conversation about basic concerns that is called dialogue. Today, when Jewish and Christian laypeople, clergy, and scholars come together to engage in dialogue, they are doing something that was almost unheard of just a generation ago. The goal of this dialogue is not to convert the other person or even to reach theological agreement; history has already seen too many demands made on Jews to conform to Christian standards. Rather the goal is to reach awareness about and generate respect for the other's deepest convictions. With knowledge, reflection, and good will, Christians may come to identify and wrestle to the ground the ambiguities within the church's tradition that have led to contempt of Jews and violations of Jesus' message.

Like much of its subject matter, this project has been difficult, but ultimately rewarding. For their confidence in my ability to accomplish it, I wish to acknowledge the support of Barry Menuez, of the division of Education for Mission and Ministry of the Episcopal Church, and Rabbi Leon Klenicki and Judith Muffs, of the Department of Interfaith Affairs at the Anti-Defamation League of B'nai B'rith. The project could not have been undertaken had I not been studying at Union Theological Seminary, in New York City, and taking courses in Jewish history and Jewish-Christian relations there and at Jewish and General Theological Seminaries. Of considerable help has been a seminarians' dialogue group sponsored by Jewish Theological Seminary and including participants from Anglican, Conservative Jewish, Orthodox Christian, Protestant, Reform Jewish, and Roman Catholic faith traditions.

3

For providing me with opportunities to try out some of these ideas in adult-education forums, I thank the Revs. Guthrie Speers and Margaret Ferguson of the First Presbyterian Church of New Canaan, Connecticut, and the Revs. Priscilla Williams and Douglas Wigner of St. John's Episcopal Church of Stamford, Connecticut. Leah Ruth Robinson has been the most helpful and encouraging of critics.

After I completed the manuscript in May 1987, it passed through the hands of several editors, among them Jim Carpenter and Leon Klenicki. They made no additions and only a few small deletions. Their sole significant change was to move the section on worship to the appendix from my original position for it as Chapter I. Worship is of such importance for religious people that I thought it best to open the book with the extraordinary story of how the early Christians borrowed so much of their liturgy from ancient Jewish practices. Once we note the deep similarities (and differences) in that crucial area, we will readily note them in other parts of the dialogue.

Stamford, Connecticut
June 8, 1991

I. Jews and Christians in the First Century

Anti-Judaism and antisemitism are not products of the twentieth century, or even of the second century, for when the church father Justin Martyr referred in about 150 C.E. to "the senseless Jews," he was not the first Christian to attack Jews.[1] Portions of the Christian scriptures themselves can be read as an anti-Judaic tract in the extreme. For example, in the eighth chapter of the gospel according to John, the evangelist portrays Jesus arguing with some Jews in the temple:

> You are of your father the devil, and your will is to do your father's desires. He was a murderer from the beginning, and has nothing to do with the truth, because there is no truth in him (Jn 8:44).

Those are shocking words for people living in the shadow of Auschwitz. Did Jesus actually say them? Even if he did not, what are Christians to make of such a statement in their own scripture? If Christians today accept its apparent reasoning, they like many Christians before them (including the evangelist), can only conclude that Jews are enemies. But if they reject it out of hand, they may be compromising our scriptural heritage.

In this chapter we will try to address that dilemma as we look at attitudes about Judaism in the Christian scriptures in the context of Jewish and Christian history in Palestine during the first century C.E. Jewish-Christian relations in those crucial years break down into two periods, separated by the watershed event of the destruction of the second temple in 70 C.E., and which are reflected by two distinct types of literature in the Christian scriptures. In summary, these are the characteristics of those two periods:

5

Period 1: before 70. Palestinian Judaism was diverse, but for many Jews—which included the first generation of Jesus-followers—the Temple remained the center of worship. Paul, the apostle to the Gentiles in Greece and Asia Minor, wrote letters arguing that Gentile Christians need not observe the laws of the Torah and that despite their opposition to Jesus, Jews not only were saved but played a vital role in the salvation of Christians.

Period 2: after 70. After the Romans destroyed the temple, Palestinian Judaism went through a period of reconstruction, during which many Jesus-followers voluntarily left or were expelled from synagogues in order to form their own organizations. The gospels probably were written about this time, and some of the stories about Jesus and certain of his words almost certainly reflect these late first century tensions in anti-Judaic ways.

Because of a scarcity of sources, there is still much that is not known about this extremely important period in the histories of both Christianity and Judaism. Many of the questions raised about this time go unanswered, and probably will remain unanswered forever unless the dry deserts and caves of Israel and Egypt loosen their grasp on documents that will tell us more about the people and events of the time when one faith community was born, and another was transformed.

1. "THE TEACHING OF CONTEMPT"

Before we begin, let us define some essential terms. "Anti-Judaism" and "antisemitism" are the two types of prejudice *against Jews simply because they are Jews* and not because of anything that Jews have done. While they share both a contempt for Jews as a people and a systematic program of teaching that contempt, the two "isms" differ in some important ways.

Antisemitism is often called "racial antisemitism" because it is founded on a conviction that Semites—a term for "Jews" that is derived from Noah's son Shem (Gen 10:21–31)—are genetically inferior to non-Jews. Antisemites believe that Jews must be separated or even eradicated before they spread their weaknesses to Gentiles (non-Jews). Although scholars have found traces of racial antisemitism in ancient times, it began to flourish in the nineteenth century and thrived in our century, most notably under Adolf Hitler.

Anti-Judaism, the other type of prejudice, is often called "theological anti-Judaism" because its argument is founded on theological rather than racial grounds. People who are prejudiced with anti-Judaism deny rights and recognition to Jews who have not converted to Christianity. These people believe that Jews are to be held in contempt because of their disbelief in Jesus Christ as messiah and savior. Even more important, Jews are to be punished as a collectivity because "they killed Jesus." According to this notion of prejudice, no matter how few Jews played a part in the crucifixion (and no matter what role was played by Pontius Pilate), *all Jews* who lived then and have lived since are collectively responsible for Jesus' execution.

In this book, most of our work will concern theological prejudice against Jews. Anti-Judaism may at first appear to be much more tolerant than the virulent antisemitism that produced the obscenity of the holocaust. Unlike Hitler, the church has generally refused to initiate systematic destruction of all Jews. Humiliation, segregation, and conversion, yes; genocide, no. Yet as we will see, the Christian church has, throughout its history, not only restricted Jewish religious and secular life, but also provided the vocabulary and rationale for savage persecutions.

Three key ingredients of anti-Judaism are the following misapprehensions about the early history of Christians and their relations with Jews. They are either found in the Christian scriptures or are derived from a particular interpretation of them.

1. Judaism in the days of Jesus and the apostles was monolithic and intolerant.
2. Jesus and the apostles practiced a radically new kind of religion that completely rejected Judaism and Jews.
3. "The Jews killed Jesus": all Jews were and continue to be responsible for the death of Jesus.

In this chapter we will address each of these topics as we look at the Christian scriptures and their context in the first century.

2. THE JEWISH CONTEXT

We must not forget that for most of the first century, almost all followers of Jesus in Palestine and Syria (where the gospels were written) were Jews, just as were their leader and his mother Mary. If they were typical of the age, they were a varied lot. Far from being monolithic, Judaism was extremely diverse, with a wide range of concerns and goals anchored in a richly textured tradition. People who professed to be Jews honored the Torah and, while it remained standing, the temple in Jerusalem, and they observed the festivals of the Jewish calendar. But they differed greatly in styles of life, on how the Torah should be interpreted for their own times, on whether their leaders should be priests or laypeople, and on how God should be worshiped. It is not too much of an exaggeration to say that first century Judaism was almost as pluralistic as twentieth century American Christianity.

In the time of Jesus, the Jews of Palestine (the Roman term for the area formerly known as Israel) were roughly divided into four very different groups: Pharisees, Sadducees, Zealots, and Essenes. The last two differed the most radically. The Zealots were nationalists and revolutionaries who led the disastrous revolt against Rome in which the temple was destroyed in 70 C.E. The Essenes were a rigorously ascetic group of a mystical bent who retreated into the wilderness; for Christians, their main influence may have been their initiation ceremony, which was baptism. These two groups—the Zealots looking for salvation in political action and the Essenes seeking it in monastic reflection—were, scholars tell us, relatively less influential in the daily life of the Jew of Jesus' day than the others, upon whom we will focus here.

The most important groups in mainline Judaism were the Sadducees and the Pharisees, who are mentioned in the gospels and the Acts of the Apostles as the opponents of Jesus and his followers (see, for example, Mt 22). These two groups differed in basic understandings of the essence of Judaism; the Christian scriptures sometimes (but not always) reflect these differences. The main variation lay in their stress on the foundational elements of Judaism. Simon the Just, a third century B.C.E. high priest, said that the Jewish faith rested on the "three-legged stool" of Torah, temple sacrifice, and acts of charity. The Sadducees and Pharisees each stressed one of the first two legs—the Sadducees the temple, and the Pharisees the law—and agreed on the third.

The Sadducees were adherents of the temple, daily sacrifice, and the priests who served them. Their history parallels that of the second temple. When they returned from the Babylonian exile in about 538 B.C.E., Jews rebuilt Solomon's temple, which had been destroyed in the Babylonian war of conquest. Daily sacrifice was reestablished in the midst of a movement led by Nehemiah and Ezra. The two most important elements in this movement were, first, a literal interpretation of the law as it was laid down in the Torah and, second, a keen nationalism demonstrated most vividly in the book of Esther, whose events are still celebrated in the festival of Purim.

Like all such movements, this one went through a cycle of wavering and strengthening. Its most fervent revival came during and after the Maccabean revolt of 168–165 B.C.E., which is described in the four books of the Maccabees. (These books are apocryphal—not part of the canon of scripture—in Protestant and Jewish Bibles, while the Roman Catholic Old Testament includes 1 and 2 Maccabees.) The Maccabees and their followers revolted against the militantly anti-Jewish Syrian ruler Antiochus IV, who banned circumcision and ordered all Jews to worship the Greek god Zeus. He profaned the temple by raising a statue of Zeus in the sanctuary and—most shockingly—placed pig meat on the sacrificial altar. This appalling "desolating sacrilege" (1 Mac 1:54, Dan 11:31, Mk 13:1) was the last straw. The Jews rose up in a revolt led by a man named Mattathias and his son Judas, called Judas Maccabeus (or "Judas the hammerer"). One of Judas' first acts after overthrowing Antiochus was to order the cleansing and rededication of the temple (1 Mac 4:36–61). Jews today celebrate this event in the early winter festival called Hanukkah, the festival of lights, with its elegant menorah.

The functionaries in the cleansing of the temple were the Sadducees. Their name probably was derived from Zadok, the chief priest when Solomon built the first temple in approximately 1000 B.C.E. The Sadducees dominated Jewish leadership for many years after the Maccabean revolt. They were closely identified with the priests who performed the daily sacrifices in the temple in Jerusalem and with the high priest appointed by the Roman authorities. What is known of their beliefs suggests that they did not believe in resurrection (see Mt 22:23) and argued for a strict observance of the Torah allowing little room for interpretation to suit contemporary needs.

The Pharisees differed from the Sadducees by stressing the synagogue and a somewhat more flexible interpretation of Torah. The synagogue—or assembly of Jews around the Torah readings—was not a new institution, but this kind of worship seems to have become more pronounced around the time of the Maccabean revolt. A group of scribes (educated Jews) called the *Hasidim,* or "pious ones," gathered separately; they eventually became known as the Pharisees, possibly because the word is derived from one meaning "separate." While they observed the Torah, they were more open than the Sadducees to the possibility of supplanting the written law with oral interpretation in order to make the

Torah more relevant to contemporary life. For example, where the Torah forbade self-defense on the sabbath, oral interpretation permitted it. Unlike the Sadducees, the Pharisees believed in the physical resurrection of the dead. They were often associated with teachers and transcribers of the Torah called scribes.

The Christian scriptures often portray the Pharisees and scribes as foils for Jesus' teaching. Yet we should not be too quick to judge harshly, as two examples found in Matthew's gospel indicate. Early, during the sermon on the mount, Jesus says that nobody can enter the kingdom of heaven without being righteous beyond the standard of the scribes and Pharisees (Mt 5:20). Rather than a criticism of law-abiding Jews, this statement actually sets a high standard indeed, for Jesus has just said that "not an iota, not a dot, will pass away from the law until all is accomplished" and that anybody who eases up on interpreting the commandments "shall be called least in the kingdom of heaven" (Mt 5:18–19).

The most vivid attack on the Pharisees and scribes appears at much greater length in Matthew 23, where Jesus is represented as berating them for their hypocrisy and pride: "Woe to you, scribes and Pharisees!" This saying probably echoes convictions that were prominent within the Jewish community.[2]

One of the most important Pharisees was Hillel (c. 50 B.C.E.–20 C.E.), a teacher who had come to Palestine from Mesopotamia, where the descendants of the Babylonian exiles lived. While he by no means ignored the laws concerning circumcision, food, purity, and the sabbath, Hillel placed a very high priority on the law's humaneness. After his death, his followers preserved many of his ideas in the rabbinic commentaries on the Torah called the Talmud, which will be examined in greater detail later on. One of his most famous sayings was his golden rule, "What is hateful to you, do not to your fellow-creature."[3] Jesus rephrased this as, "Whatever you wish that men would do to you, do so to them" (Mt 7:12).

By the mid-first century C.E. Jews came to apply the title rabbi, "teacher," to Hillel and his followers. Rabbis were scholars who interpreted the law for their communities and so became community leaders. They also were teachers. The greater rabbis, such as Hillel and his contemporary Shammai, headed schools where they debated over the Torah and the meaning of life and the afterlife. The following statement in the Talmud gives a good idea of the mixture of philosophy and practicality that flavored these debates:

The Schools of Hillel and Shammai disputed two and a half years whether it would have been better if man had or had not been created. Finally they agreed that it would have been better had he not been created, but since he had been created, let him investigate his past doings, and let him examine what he is about to do.[4]

The rabbis were not compensated for their services, for many held that the Torah was too important that someone be paid to interpret it. But they were important people. In the Acts of the Apostles we read of Hillel's son, "the Pharisee in the council named Gamaliel," who defended the apostles' right to preach in the sanhedrin, the Jews' ruling council in Jerusalem (Acts 6:34).

The rise of the rabbis did not mean the end of the temple priesthood, and the high priest and his subordinates continued to have many responsibilities until the foundation of their existence, the temple itself, was destroyed in 70 C.E. Even after that, the priests were counted on to determine the Jewish calendar, that is, when the sabbath, holy days, and festivals began and ended with the new moon or with evening.

3. THE FIRST GENERATION CHRISTIANS AND JUDAISM

Where did the first generation of Christians fit into this scene? Naturally, like any group of people assembled in community around a new belief, they were quite insecure. Despite occasional statements to the contrary in the Christian scriptures and in church histories, the early church did not find its way easily. Not only did many Jews resist the "good news" that the messiah had come, died, and been resurrected, but the apostles were by no means unified among themselves about how Jesus' message should be acted out.

The most controversial issue was the relationship of the Torah to the new faith: should Jewish and Gentile converts have to obey the dietary and other requirements of the Torah? This issue was debated heatedly by Peter, James, Barnabas, and Paul in the apostolic council in 48 C.E. (Acts 15). Apparently that did not put an end to the issue, for Paul, the appointed missionary to the Gentiles (non-Jews), argued it all over again in a letter that he wrote in about 53 to a Christian community in a part of Asia Minor called Galatia.

Besides their internal squabbles, the early Christians inevitably had struggles with opponents, among them proselytizing Jews who did not like competing with them in the search for potential Gentile converts. Paul, the first Christian writer, addressed this issue with typical frankness. The Jews, he wrote to the Thessalonians in about 50 C.E., "drove us out, and displease God and oppose all men by hindering us from speaking to the Gentiles that they may be saved" (1 Thes 2:16).

This Paul probably was the earliest Christian author whose writings survive. He was a Jew born and raised as a Pharisee who had persecuted Jesus-followers, but who was dramatically converted in 35 C.E. (Gal 1:13–17). He took on a mission to preach the *gospel* ("good news") of the dramatic circumstances of Jesus' life and death. For the rest of his life, during thousands of miles of arduous travels, he told the simple but extraordinary story of how a man died for humanity's sins and then was resurrected (1 Cor 15:3–4), and it changed the lives of many.

Taking on a ministry to the Gentiles, Paul spent very little time in Palestine but rather traveled extensively in Asia Minor and Greece, whose Christians he inspired, chided, and instructed in person and in long letters. He and his followers circulated the letters to other Christian churches. These letters helped bind Christians together into a close-knit international community. It is likely that the Christian scriptures contain only some of Paul's letters, and those were written in the relatively short period between about 48 and 56 C.E., before Paul was arrested and taken to Rome presumably to be executed about 60 C.E. (Scholars believe that some of the letters ascribed to Paul—for example, 2 Thessalonians, Ephesians, and 1 and 2 Timothy—probably were written by his followers in his name.)

The problem that attracted (even obsessed) Paul throughout the letters in the Christian scriptures was the one of the relationship between Judaism and the new faith, in particular the question as to what one should have to do in order to be justified before God. The issue was whether a Jesus-follower was meant to observe the dietary, behavioral, and other regulations laid down in the Torah. Paul's reflections on these problems are by no means clear or consistent, as the author of the second letter of Peter complained when he wrote, "There are some things in them hard to understand, which the ignorant and unstable twist to their own destruction, as they do with other scriptures" (2 Pet 3:16; Professor Raymond E. Brown of Union Theological Seminary has called this verse "the understatement of the New Testament"). At times Paul seems to be saying that Jews have lost the right to exist as a faith (1 Thes 2:14–16) and that Torah has lost all validity (Gal 3:19–20). On the other hand, in his last letter, which he wrote to the Christians in Rome, he concluded that though "Christ is the end [or culmination] of the law" (Rom 10:4) God did not reject "his people" the Jews (Rom 11:1). The Jews play a vital part in God's plan, for their rejection of Jesus only leads the Gentiles to him. After all the Gentiles are converted, so too will the Jews (Rom 11:11–24).

Noting these contradictions, one New Testament scholar, W. D. Davies, has stressed Paul's "tumultuous, tortuous nature."[5] No doubt Paul's doubts derived from two sources: first, his radical conversion from Jewish persecutor of Christians to Christian missionary; second, his conviction (which he shared with many other Jesus-followers) that the second coming of Jesus (the *parousia*) that would herald the end of the world would occur imminently. Yet Paul clearly and consistently believed one thing: we are justified through the grace of God acting through Jesus Christ, not by anything that we do (Gal 2:15–21), and it is a conceit to boast that our own actions bring about our salvation. Faith and the grace of God are enough, for "everyone who has faith may be justified" (Rom 10:4).

One problem with Paul's letters is that in making this point, he sometimes seems to exaggerate Judaism's reliance on the precise wording of the written Torah. Perhaps he was reacting to an extreme form of legalism that he had seen or had himself practiced, or maybe he was swept up in the exaggeration that always follows in the trail of polemic. Whatever the case, many readers of his energetic defenses of the gospel have mistakenly come to the conclusion that Judaism contains no sense of divine grace and Christianity has no law.

While a Christian will be deeply moved by the power of Paul's faith, a Christian need not allow Paul's polemic to harden her or his heart against Judaism. The Hebrew scriptures are filled with God's love. We see this in the covenants with Noah, Abraham, Jacob, and Moses (Gen 8, 15–17, 28; Ex 19–20), and in the books of the prophets Amos, Hosea, and Jeremiah, where there are exemplary expressions of grace and everlasting love by God for the Jews (see Am 9; Hos 2:14–23) and a promise of "a new covenant with the house of Israel and the house of Judah" (Jer 31:31). We see God's grace in the gentle story of reconciliation in the book of Ruth, in the theme of forgiveness in the book of Jonah (where the least forgiving character is the prophet himself), and in the lovely wedding poems in the Song of Solomon, whose imagery Christians have borrowed to describe the relationship between Jesus Christ and the church.

Paul's attacks on "the law" have frequently been interpreted by Christians as proof that Christianity is free of legalisms. Not only does the sheer bulk of church canon law and denominational regulations puncture that balloon, but the Christian scriptures also offer evidence that law and Christianity are compatible. This is especially clear in Matthew's gospel. Even as he criticizes the Pharisees and scribes for being proud and hypocritical, Jesus says that his followers should do whatever the Jewish leaders say—which can only mean to observe the Torah (Mt 23:2). The sermon on the mount, in Matthew 5–7, restates the ten commandments and other parts of the Torah in the attempt to show how the law is fulfilled in the new age of the "new Moses," Jesus Christ. To quote W. D. Davies, whose little book *The Sermon on the Mount* offers a fine introduction to these issues:

> At no point in the Church, not even in Paul, who coined the phrase "Christ is the end of the Law," is there a radical rejection of the traditional law of Judaism but rather the recognition of its fulfillment in the "law of love" and in the words of Jesus.[6]

It has been said that a very good example of Jewish law, or *halakha,* is the sermon on the mount itself, and especially the section called "the antitheses" in which Jesus elaborates on the ten commandments. There Jesus interpreted the Torah much as would a rabbi like Hillel. It seems that Jesus, however, went far beyond the original text, for example: "You have heard that it was said, 'An eye for an eye and a tooth for a tooth' [Ex 21:23–24]. But I say to you, 'Do not resist one who is evil. But if any one strikes you on the right cheek, turn to him the other also' " (Mt 5:38).

Although his attacks on the centrality of the Torah have often been interpreted as denials that Jews could be saved, Paul was anything but an elitist. His universalism surfaces in many of his letters: "God has consigned all men to disobedience, that he may have mercy upon all" (Rom 11:32); "For there is no distinction between Jew and Greek; the same Lord is Lord of all and bestows his riches upon all who call upon him" (Rom 10:12); "There is neither Jew nor Greek, there is neither slave nor free, there is neither male nor female; for you are all one in Christ Jesus" (Gal 3:27–29); God "has mercy on whomever he wills, and he hardens the heart of whomever he wills" (Rom 9:18).

What a reader of Paul must keep firmly in mind is that when Paul attacked Jews for not converting, he was writing from a vantage point that is very different from that of most Christians today. He expected the parousia, the second coming, to occur imminently, within his own lifetime in fact, and his sense of urgency was intense. He hoped to prepare the world for the parousia by including everybody in salvation, and that for him meant salvation in Jesus Christ. As a universalist, he aimed for inclusion and not exclusion. This urgency affected every aspect of his gospel. For example, when the Thessalonians asked him what would happen to the dead at the parousia, Paul, relying on the Pharisaic belief in the resurrection of the dead, answered that those who had died "in Christ" would be saved along with those who were living "in Christ" (1 Thes 4:13–18).

In a vivid image, Paul likened the relationship between Jews and Christians to a live olive tree (ancient Judaism) with some dead branches (some forms of contemporary Judaism) and some wild branches that have been grafted on (Christianity). He hoped that Jews, through conversion, would be grafted back on, "for God has the power to graft them in again" (Rom 11:17–24). In other words, the Christian law, it seems, is built upon the Torah in much the same way that the oral interpretation of Pharisaism is based on it.

Of course this does not eradicate all differences between the two faiths. For Jews, to follow the Torah is to worship God, while for Christians God is worshiped in Jesus Christ. Jews do not believe that Jesus was the messiah promised in the book of Isaiah because Jesus' coming did not bring the reign of justice expected with the messianic age. Christians believe that Jesus was not only the messiah but the Son in a much more direct sense than Jews could accept. While those differences cannot be surmounted, agreeing to acknowledge and honor them allows Jews and Christians to move on to the many areas where they do agree.

4. JUDAISM RECOVERS FROM THE DESTRUCTION OF THE TEMPLE

So far we have been talking about events that took place before 70 C.E. Judaism was varied, but its basic principles were much as they had been for centuries. Jesus lived and died; some Jews were converted to the Jesus movement; there were some theological tensions between early Christians and Jews; Paul wrote his letters. After 70 C.E., however, the situation was different.

Between 66 and 73 C.E. bands of Zealots rose up in rebellion against the occupying Romans. Unlike the Maccabean revolt more than two hundred years earlier, the revolution ended in disaster. In 70 C.E. Roman forces destroyed the temple as they attacked teams of Zealots hiding there. The war ended three years later with the mass suicide of the defenders of the fortress of Masada. With the destruction of the second temple, not only was the center of Sadducee life eradicated, but apparently all Judaism stood on the brink as well. To begin to understand what the destruction of the temple meant to Jews, I would suggest that we try to picture what the total destruction of the Vatican would mean to Roman Catholics. The difference, of course, is that while the eucharist and baptism can be celebrated in any Catholic church anywhere, Jewish sacrifice could be conducted only in the temple. With the loss of temple sacrifice, which provided a direct link to the covenants with God, how could Judaism survive?

The extraordinary thing is that Judaism *did* survive the loss of the temple. The Pharisees, with their flexible theology and their use of the decentralized institution of the synagogue, were able to adapt to the catastrophe. Their leader was a pupil of Hillel named Rabbi Johanan ben Zakkai who escaped from Jerusalem before the final assault on the temple and (hidden, it was said, in a coffin) fled to a small town named Yavneh, near the seacoast. There he gathered other surviving rabbis and priests and, in difficult debates and heart-rending compromises, they hammered out a reconstructed Judaism that was based not on temple sacrifice but on the observance of *halakha* in normal everyday life. It was not easy. Recall Simon the Just's saying about the three-legged chair: Judaism was supported by temple sacrifice, the Torah, and acts of charity. How could the chair stand with only two legs? Obviously it would have to balance while the remaining leg was reinforced. The following story is told in the Talmud about Rabbi Johanan ben Zakkai:

> It happened that Rabbi Johanan ben Zakkai went out from Jerusalem, and Rabbi Joshua followed him, and he saw the burnt ruins of the Temple, and he said, "Woe is it that the place, where the sins of Israel find atonement, is laid waste." Then said Rabbi Johanan, "Grieve not, we have an atonement equal to the Temple, the doing of loving deeds," as it is said, "I desire love and not sacrifice."[7]

The reference is to the prophet Hosea, who quoted God as follows: "For I desire steadfast love and not sacrifice, the knowledge of God rather than burnt offerings" (Hos 6:6). Jesus, Matthew tells us, also used that verse, but led on to a conclusion that can be construed as being anti-Jewish:

> "I tell you, something greater than the Temple is here. And if you had known what this means, 'I desire mercy and not sacrifice,' you would not have condemned the guiltless. For the Son of Man is lord of the Sabbath" (Mt 12:6–7).

Like all reformations, the restoration of Judaism after the destruction of the second temple did not proceed comfortably. Every group whose very existence is in question will inevitably develop a conservative policy of exclusionism against its uncertain adherents. Rabbi Johanan ben Zakkai and his successors were particularly concerned about the *minim,* "heretics," a general term for all who strayed from the teachings of the Torah. In order to identify the *minim,* the rabbis wrote a blessing to be used in the daily worship services that cursed heretics. The members of the congregation took turns saying the blessings; anybody who hesitated or stumbled over the words of this blessing was assumed to be a heretic and was expelled from the synagogue.[8]

A few scholars believe that at least some Christians were considered to be among the *minim* and were identified through this blessing. Whether or not this blessing was the agent, there is evidence that synagogues expelled Jewish Jesus-followers. For example, in John's gospel there are three mentions of expulsions (Jn 9:22; 12:42; 16:2), and writing about seventy-five years later, the Christian writer Justin Martyr attacked Jews "cursing in your synagogues those that believe in Christ."[9]

This does not mean that expulsion from the synagogue meant automatic excommunication from Judaism. Neither does it mean that *all* synagogues made a policy of expelling *all* followers of Jesus, or that conversion to Christianity automatically required a believer to cease worshiping in a synagogue. In the earliest days of Christianity, a sizeable number of Jesus-followers made a point of observing the dictates of the Torah; foremost among these Jewish-Christians were Jesus' brother James and other people living in Jerusalem. They may have been the men who, the book of Acts tells us, "came down from Judea and were teaching the brethren, 'Unless you are circumcised according to the custom of Moses, you cannot be saved' " (Acts 15:1). The most important critic of these Torah-observant Christians was Paul, the apostle to the communities of Gentiles, a group that probably provided more converts to Christianity than did Jewish communities. But we should note that even Paul worshiped in the temple when he returned to Jerusalem (Acts 21:26).

While some Jewish-Christians known as Ebionites, or "the poor," were still active in the second century, the relationship between Jews and Christians soon came to be typified less by agreement than by schism. The informed debate between Christians and Jews dissolved into a bitter life-and-death struggle over the claim of who knew *the truth.* For evidence of exclusiveness on the Christian side, we need look no further than the Christian scriptures. Paul's letters make it clear that within twenty-five

years of Jesus' death, Christians outside Jerusalem were not only challenging the ancient teachings of the Torah but were even claiming that the
Jews were no longer included in God's dispensation.[10] A generation later,
the authors of the gospels included vivid criticisms of Judaism in their
stories of Jesus; John went so far as to put in Jesus' mouth the most
unlikely charge that the leaders of the Jews were children of the devil (Jn
8:44). By the middle of the second century, the Christian Justin Martyr
was accusing Jews of being so blind that they did not even understand
their own scriptures.[11]

Meanwhile, on the Jewish side the rabbis were expelling Jesus-
followers from synagogues, denouncing Christians to Roman authorities,[12] and teaching that while it was permissible to rescue Jewish writings
from a fire on the sabbath, "we do not save from a fire the gospels and the
books of the *minim*," since heretical writings were devoid of sanctity.[13]

Apparently neither side even considered the possibility that God
might work in two ways at the same time. In their claims of exclusivism,
both sides set a lasting and unfortunate example for later Jewish-Christian
relations.

5. THE CHRISTIAN REACTION

Such exclusions on the part of the synagogues did much to sustain
Jews during their time of despair. Without it, Judaism might easily have
disappeared altogether. It also helped lead to the development of Christianity as a distinct faith. Among the apostates were people called "Nazarenes" who considered themselves Jews and worshiped in the synagogues.
But they also demonstrated belief in the messiahship and even the divinity of a certain Jesus of Nazareth, who had been crucified forty or more
years earlier in Jerusalem and about whom many strange and wondrous
stories were circulating. Those stories were being written down around the
time that the rabbis were saving Judaism from the ruins of the temple, and
it was inevitable that the expulsions and the Jewish-Christian tensions
that surrounded them were reflected in these writings, particularly in
Matthew and John.

Although their authors tended to claim that they were accurate, objective biographies of Jesus, the four gospels are much more than mere
collections of biographical detail. First of all, while the authors were of
course concerned with facts, their primary goal undoubtedly was to pass
on to their readers the God-given inspiration that had moved them to

become followers of Jesus Christ in the first place. Facts in the scientific, objective meaning of the term as we understand it today were secondary to inspiration. Second, because the stories had been circulating orally for several decades before they were written down, they naturally acquired certain traits from other popular stories of the time that may have highly dramatized and otherwise enhanced the already dramatic original.

Third and probably most important, the authors were writing from a particular situation that was shaped by the very events they were describing. Like any story-teller, they told their stories from a point of view reflecting that situation. This kind of bias is inevitable with historical writing. The difference is that while modern-day scholars work hard to identify and discipline their prejudices, writers whose orientation is not scholarly but inspirational will write *through* their prejudices instead of *around* them.

The authors of the gospels fall into the second group. To them, the story of Jesus was not over; it was living history. In the communities and Christian churches around them, in their eucharists and their baptisms, in their disputes with their neighbors and among themselves, wherever they looked in the struggling, new communities, these authors saw that no matter how they told Jesus' story, they were also telling the story of their faith communities.

In other words, the gospels can be read on two levels. The narratives tell the story of events that occurred at about 30 C.E., in the time of Jesus. The details often describe what was going on in the communities of the authors thirty to sixty years later. The first story concerns Jesus' life, about which there were few controversies. The second concerns how to interpret that life: Was he human? Messiah? Son of God? About this there were many, very deep, and very violent debates.

Two examples of this intrusion of the writer's point of view into the story of Jesus are found in the account of the healing of the blind man in the ninth chapter of John's gospel and in the ascription of responsibility for Jesus' death that all four gospels give to Jews, "rulers and elders" in the synoptics, and *the* Jews in the fourth gospel.

THE MEANING OF "THE JEWS" IN JOHN 9[14]

In John 9 Jesus cures a beggar of his blindness on the sabbath. The beggar is taken to the Pharisees, some of whom complain that Jesus cannot possibly be from God because he violated the sabbath by working on it. They then ask the beggar's parents whether he was blind in the first place. The parents are frightened that they might be expelled from the synagogue if they verify the miracle, so they tell the doubters to ask their son. The beggar does all he can to convince them that a miracle has actually occurred; he is rewarded for his pains by being cast out of the synagogue. In the last verse, Jesus tells the doubting Pharisees that they are guilty as hypocrites because they know full well not only that the blind man was cured but also that he, Jesus, is from God. John's story leaves the reader with feelings of sympathy for the blind man, contempt for the synagogue leaders, and faithful respect for Jesus' intolerance of stupid regulations.

But there is something in John's story that should give us pause. This element is the qualification that John applies to the term "the Jews." When we use that word today, we generally mean *all* Jews. That John may have meant something else is suggested by the fact that the beggar's father and mother refer to "the Jews" as other people even though the parents themselves obviously are Jewish (what else could they be if they are concerned about being expelled from the synagogue?). For John, the term "the Jews" seems to mean "all Jews who do not believe in Jesus and hate Christians." Later in the gospel Jesus says of the Jews, "They will put you out of the synagogue; indeed, the hour is coming when whoever kills you is offering service to God" (Jn 16:2). As Raymond E. Brown has pointed out, in later Jewish-Christian relations "tragically . . . the situation of John 16:2 was reversed, and Christians put Jews to death thinking they were thus serving God."[15]

All this suggests that John used this formula "the Jews" in two ways, one of them historically as "Jesus' opponents in the Jewish community" and the other as "people who expel or persecute Christians today." The persecutors probably are "the Jews" who are damned as being of the devil in John 8:44. In the fourth gospel the primary concern literally from the first word is to proclaim Jesus' divinity. Therefore, anybody who rejected or even doubted that Jesus was the Son of God was on the devil's side.

The evangelist's anti-Judaism is regrettable. But "tragic" is the only word to describe the inability or unwillingness of Christians to acknowledge that John's situation is not theirs. All too often, Christians have applied the terrible epithet of John 8:44 to Jews everywhere. To quote one biblical scholar, Professor John Koenig of General Theological Seminary, "The Fourth Gospel becomes antisemitic whenever it is read or taught in such a way as to suggest that our attitude toward Jews ought to be the same as the author's."[16]

DID THE JEWS KILL JESUS?

One reason why "theological anti-Judaism" has survived is that the New Testament says in several places that "the Jews"—all Jews—are responsible for Jesus' death. Read, for example, what Paul wrote to the Thessalonians: "You suffered the same things from your own countrymen as they did from the Jews, who killed both the Lord Jesus and the prophets. . . . But God's wrath has come upon them at last!" (1 Thes 2:14–16).[17]

The sense of betrayal remained strong for centuries. Until quite recently, in Roman Catholic services on Good Friday a prayer was said for the Jews, using an adjective that means "treacherous" and "faithless." The congregation was bidden to pray for the perfidious Jews, that God might remove the veil from their hearts so that they too might acknowledge Jesus Christ.[18] The prayer was said without the usual genuflection because, according to Christian tradition, this would duplicate the mocking genuflection made during the scourging of Jesus.[19]

It took the story-tellers who wrote the gospels to add the other parts and the blame. The authors of the gospels made the Roman procurator Pontius Pilate a sympathetic character who unwillingly gave in to the pressure of the Jewish sanhedrin—the group of seventy-one Jews who ruled on *halakhic* matters—to turn Jesus over to be crucified. According to Matthew and Mark, Pilate perceived the Jewish leaders' motivation to be envy of Jesus. But the main source of the idea that *the* Jews killed Jesus is John's gospel, which is also the most influential passion account. It is the one usually read and sung on Good Friday, the day when Christians are most sensitive to the narrative. John even portrays Pilate as believing in Jesus' kingship over the Jews and of being opposed to his execution. The crucifixion takes place only because "the Jews" insist on imposing the penalty on blasphemers that was required by the Torah (Jn 18–19; Lev 24:16). For John the issue was one of collective guilt: the Jews were deicides—God-killers.

Christians have become so accustomed to the strong anti-Judaic themes of John's passion story that they often ignore the other versions, which give accounts that undermine the theory of Jewish collective guilt.

For example, Mark and Matthew rather carefully lay the blame for instigating the recommendation for the death sentence solely on the chief priests and their intimate followers. Unlike John, they do not specifically identify as Jews the crowd that demands "Crucify him!" (Mk 14–15; Mt 27). Luke goes so far as to present a sympathetic Pharisee who acknowledges Jesus as teacher and tries to warn him away from the promising trouble (Lk 19:30).

A convincing critique of the deicide charge leveled against all Jews is the body of evidence from outside the gospels indicating that some events said to have taken place on that day in 30 or 31 C.E. are invented. Other than the testimony of the gospels and the account of the execution of James (which will be discussed later on), there is no evidence anywhere of the sanhedrin condemning anybody to death. Only the Roman procurator had that right, which he used to keep public order. If the Jews who were most opposed to Jesus—the chief priests, who were appointed by the procurator—were upset with this obstinate Galilean prophet, with all his talk about the destruction of the temple, all they had to do to get Pilate's ear was to claim that Jesus was making trouble. That they did. But Pilate's approval was necessary if their wish to put Jesus out of the picture was to become reality.

Therefore, while *a few* Jews may have had *some* responsibility for the death of the Jew Jesus, not all Jews had all responsibility. To hold *all* Jews—then and since—responsible would be the equivalent of holding all men named Peter responsible for the apostle's denial of Jesus in the courtyard. If Christians have learned to forgive Peter for his betrayal, then Christians should be able to read the passion stories with some respect for facts.

The deicide charge, so thoroughly engrained in Christian antisemitism, is a topic to which we will return in greater detail later on. Here let us simply ask why this story has been so thoroughly and widely believed for almost two thousand years.

One explanation for the widespread belief that "the Jews killed Jesus" develops a theme that we have introduced earlier: the people who wrote down these stories in the years between about 50 and 100 C.E. read their present into the past. Although the main threats to Jesus and his followers around 30 C.E. were the local officials of the Roman empire, twenty and more years later the Jews, not the empire, posed the greatest challenge to the Jesus-followers. Writing at that time, and fighting the battles around synagogue membership and theology, the authors of the gospels found it hard to resist the temptation to tell their stories with

Jewish, not Roman, villains. And so they wrote—and for centuries Christians have believed—the fiction that the Jews, not the Romans, killed Jesus.[20]

NOTES

1. Justin Martyr, *First Apology,* in *The Ante-Nicene Fathers,* A. Cleveland Coxe, ed. (Grand Rapids: Eerdmans, 1981), vol. I, chap. 63.

2. Cf. Claude G. Montefiore and H. Loewe, eds., *A Rabbinic Anthology* (New York: Schocken, 1974), p. 488.

3. Sab. 31a, in Montefiore and Loewe, *op. cit.,* p. 173.

4. 'Erub. 13b, in *ibid.,* p. 539.

5. Davies warns that Paul's confusion "should make us chary of making his experience in any way normative." W.D. Davies, *The Setting of the Sermon on the Mount* (Cambridge: Cambridge University Press, 1964), p. 155.

6. *Ibid.,* p. 154.

7. Aboth de R. Nathan, IV, IIa, in Montefiore and Loewe, *op. cit.,* p. 431.

8. Cf. Reuven Kimelman, "*Birkat ha-Minim* and the Lack of Evidence for an Anti-Jewish Christian Prayer in Late Antiquity," in E.P. Sanders, ed., *Jewish and Christian Self-Definition* (Philadelphia: Fortress, 1981), vol. II, pp. 226–244.

9. Justin Martyr, *Dialogue with Trypho,* in *The Ante-Nicene Fathers,* A. Cleveland Coxe, ed. (Grand Rapids: Eerdmans, 1981), vol. I, chap. 16.

10. See especially Paul's letter to the Galatians, and chapters 9, 10, and 11 of his letter to the Romans.

11. Justin Martyr, *Dialogue with Trypho,* chap. 34.

12. Raymond E. Brown, *The Community of the Beloved Disciple* (New York: Paulist, 1979), pp. 42–43.

13. Tosefta Shabbat, 13 (14).5, in Lawrence H. Schiffman, "At the Crossroads: Tannaitic Perspectives on the Jewish-Christian Schism," in E.P. Sanders, *Jewish and Christian Self-Definition,* vol. II, p. 153.

14. Cf. J. Louis Martyn, *History and Theology in the Fourth Gospel.*

15. Raymond E. Brown, *op. cit.,* p. 68.

16. John Koenig, *Jews and Christians in Dialogue: New Testament Foundations* (Philadelphia: Westminster, 1979), p. 131.

17. Some scholars believe that these verses were not actually written by Paul but added by an editor.

18. Mary Kelly, "The Good Friday Liturgy and the Jews," in *Christian-Jewish Relations* (1984), p. 17.

19. Edward H. Flannery, *The Anguish of the Jews* (New York/Mahwah: Paulist Press, A Stimulus Book, 1985 rev.), p. 87.

20. For a thorough discussion of the legal issues of Jesus' trial that exculpates the Jews from guilt for the execution, cf. Paul Winter, *On the Trial of Jesus* (Berlin: De Gruyter, 1974[2]), chaps. 6–10.

II. Rabbinic Judaism and Early Christianity: Confrontation and Rivalry

So far we have seen that the origins of Christian-Jewish relations contained their own paradoxes. Since the insecure beginnings of the new faith in the middle of the first century C.E., Christians have honored Judaism by explicitly borrowing not only the Jewish scriptures but also Jewish prayers, symbols, and structures of worship. And yet the people who wrote the Christian scriptures, and their early readers, were highly ambivalent about—and at times even antagonistic toward—the parent faith, which on occasion responded defensively.

Unfortunately, events in the early joint history of the two faiths did not allow much room for reconciliation. We will here look at how Christians appropriated the Jewish scriptures for their own purposes, while Jews developed oral interpretation of Torah in the great commentary called the Talmud. Later on we will see how Gentiles dealt with Jews.

1. TWO REBELLIONS

We have already seen how at the time of the destruction of the second temple Rabbi Johanan ben Zakkai and other rabbis formed a community at Yavneh and developed a Judaism without the temple—indeed without even a Jerusalem, where the Romans made Jews unwelcome. With a flexibility and practicality inherited from centuries of life as outsiders and from the struggles of the Babylonian exile, spiritual and community leaders succeeded in sustaining Jewish identity and tradition outside a temple-centered cult, an accomplishment of a very high order.

Of the original four parties—Pharisees, Sadducees, Zealots, and Essenes—only the Pharisees continued to play an important role in Jewish life. The more literalist party of the Sadducees had structured their life around the temple, and when the temple was destroyed, the focus of their activity was no more. The Zealots, who had been the most politically active party, had been decimated during the revolutionary war of 66–73 C.E., which they had led; the last of the Zealot leaders had died in the mass suicide in the mountaintop fortress of Masada in 73. Little is known about the Essenes; the fact that they were monastics who practiced celibacy suggests that they were far removed from the daily life of most Jews.

So Pharisees were the most active people after the fall of the temple. That was a good and probably inevitable turn of events; they had already shown themselves to be extremely practical and flexible, and if those qualities were important before 70, they were invaluable afterward.

Nevertheless, nationalistic fervor was not ended when the Zealots and the second temple were destroyed in the early 70s. Few if any peoples under the relatively benign rule of the Romans were so stubbornly independent as the Jews, who had a long revolutionary tradition that reached back to the successful Maccabean rebellion of the second century B.C.E. Following the death of King Herod the Great in 4 C.E., a short-lived but bloody revolt sprang up in Judea and in the northern district of Galilee, where it was led by a man named Judah; the Romans put it down only with the crucifixion of some two thousand rebels. The imperial census of 6 C.E. (possibly 7 C.E.) that, Luke tells us, brought Joseph and Mary to Bethlehem stimulated another rebellion in the name of Galilean nationalism led by Judah. Twenty years later, the Roman procurator Pontius Pilate (ruled 26–36) made a policy of ruthlessly executing any Galilean nationalist he could get his hands on, often without trial (e.g., cf. Lk 13:1ff). One example of the authorities' nervousness was the quick and violent reaction to some criticism of the tetrarch of Galilee, Antipas (also known as Herod). When a wandering prophet and baptizer named John said it was wrong for him to marry his niece, Antipas cut off his accuser's head (Mk 6:14–29).

These were, then, disorderly times. After the failed rebellion of 66–73 C.E., it took two more great uprisings before the Jews of the Middle East were forced to recognize that they no longer had much control over their own destiny.

The first of these revolts occurred between 115 and 117 in the diaspora, or dispersion (Mesopotamia, Egypt, Syria, and other areas outside Palestine). Choosing a moment during which the Roman emperor Trajan was distracted with a war in Mesopotamia and with his personal ambition to duplicate Alexander the Great's march of conquest toward India, Jews in Egypt and the island of Cyprus rose up. The revolt eventually spread to Mesopotamia, but for reasons that are unclear it did not appear in Palestine, even though there is some evidence that messianic expectations stimulated the rebellion. At least the Christian historian Eusebius, no friend of the Jews, referred to a leader of the Egyptian revolt as a "king" named Lucus.[1] In any case, the battles had all the violence that is usually associated with messianic rebellions. One contemporary report claimed that a red tide of blood flowed across the Mediterranean from Alexandria to Cyprus; another said that 240,000 non-Jews were killed on Cyprus.

The violence of the revolt of 115–117 was reflected in two laws and a custom that survived it. For more than a century, Jews were forbidden from immigrating to Cyprus; Palestinian Jews were so affected by the terrible news from the diaspora that they prohibited the study of Greek, the international language of the eastern empire; and in the Egyptian town of Oxyrhynchus, until as late as 200 C.E., Gentiles held a festival commemorating a victory over the Jews.

Almost twenty years after the revolts in the diaspora, Palestine itself was torn by an even more violent and, in the end, disastrously ill-fated revolution by Jews against the empire. It is known as the Bar Kokhba War, in honor of the nickname of the rebellion's leader. The background is not entirely clear, but what is known makes this a classic example of wretchedly insensitive, ignorant behavior by non-Jews toward Jews.

The trigger for the revolt seems to have been the widespread belief among Palestinian Jews that the Roman empire was ending its long-standing policy of complete religious toleration of Judaism. Julius Caesar had long ago declared Judaism a *religio licta*—a legal religion—and had given to Jews freedoms and privileges unheard of by other minority groups. Not only were Jews not required to offer sacrifice to the emperor or serve in the imperial military, but in the years when the temple was still in existence they were granted an exemption from a law that prohibited international trade in precious metals—this so that Jews in the diaspora could contribute to the upkeep of the temple through the annual temple tax.

Why the Roman empire was so tolerant of Judaism remains an open question. One reason probably was that Jews were relatively powerless. They were so few—perhaps about seven percent of the empire, four or five million in all—and so scattered—about seventy-five percent of them lived in the dispersion—that as an organized political and military force they were not an issue to the empire.

Another acceptable reason why the pagan empire let Jews alone was because Jews' concern for the world, respect for ethical behavior, and affection for order met with understanding if not high regard in Rome (although Romans found circumcision distasteful). This could not be said of Christians, whose secretiveness, mysterious liturgies, and ardor for martyrdom were strikingly alien to Roman practicality. As a rule, the empire was tolerant of any idea so long as its proponents met two conditions: first, they must acknowledge Roman rule; second, they must not be disruptive. Jews met the first rule when they did not stage nationalistic rebellions, and the second if they did not attempt to convert pagans to their faith.

To a great extent, both of these conditions reflected Roman concern for political control of Palestine, which was crucial to the empire because it lay across important trade routes. When Jews sought converts in and around Palestine, the empire felt threatened for reasons clearly explained by the historian E. Mary Smallwood in her fine book *The Jews under Roman Rule:*

> In Palestine the Jewish religion was not a harmless racial eccentricity but a politically subversive force from the viewpoint of Rome as the occupying and governing power, because it was inextricably bound up with the nationalist aspirations which sprang from militant Jewish messianism. For the Jews resident in their own land religion and nationalism were the two faces of the same coin.[2]

With one important exception, all of these reasons for toleration held true until the empire became Christian in the fourth century. The exception was the reign of the emperor Hadrian in the 130s of the common era.

At that time the Jews of Palestine began to feel severely threatened by rumors about imperial policy. The emperor Hadrian adopted the title of Jupiter, the supreme Roman deity. It was reported that while touring Palestine he announced not only that he wished to change the name of Jerusalem to a Latin name that honored Jupiter but also that he intended to raise a temple to Jupiter on the ruins of the Jewish temple. Even worse, Jews heard that circumcision was banned throughout the empire. Whether any or all of these rumors were true remains an open and probably irrelevant question, since what is important was that thousands of Jews believed them.

The argument could be made that Hadrian was not out to get Jews. The prohibition of circumcision reflected the Romans' repulsion felt toward the act, which they viewed as akin to castration, and in any case it was applied universally to Arabs, Gentiles, and Jews. The paganization of Jerusalem may have been motivated by a desire to neutralize growing religious tensions in the city, where Christians were becoming more numerous and aggressive in search of converts.

But even if the emperor was not blatantly bigoted, he showed the classic symptoms of unconscious anti-Judaism (what we today call "polite antisemitism") by being either unbelievably ignorant about or incredibly insensitive to what it meant to be a Jew. To quote E. Mary Smallwood, where the policy of paganizing the name of David's Mount Zion "betrayed a total failure to appreciate Jewish feelings about Jerusalem," the proposal to ban circumcision "cut at the very roots of Judaism."[3] Then and today, any non-Jew who took the trouble to discover the most basic Jewish customs should be aware of the crucial importance of circumcision as the seal of the covenant (see Gen 17:9–10). Likewise, anyone with even the most casual acquaintance with Jewish history and tradition would know that Hadrian's choice of names for the city reeked of the first out-and-out persecution of the Jews: the "desolating sacrilege" of 168 B.C.E., when Antiochus IV raised a statue to Zeus—Jupiter's name in Greek—in the temple (see 1 Mac 1:41–64).

These policies sparked the half-consumed kindling of rebellion left over from the diaspora rebellions of 115–117. In 132 a leader appeared. His real name was Simon, and he lived in Cozeba, and he believed himself to be the messiah as foretold in the oracle of Balaam in the Torah:

I see him, but not now; I behold him, but not nigh; a star shall come forth out of Jacob, and a sceptre shall rise out of Israel; it shall crush the forehead of Moab, and break down all the sons of Sheth (Num 24:17).

If, as was commonly understood, King David was "the star" with a royal scepter who created the nation of Israel by conquering the Moabites and the Edomites ("the sons of Sheth"), then David's successor would be his son (2 Sam 8:2, 13–14). Therefore, the name chosen for (or assumed by) Simon was Bar Kokhba, "son of the star."

With the backing of one of the most prominent rabbis, Akiba, Simon gathered a small army in 132. At first there was a series of triumphs for the Jews. For example, they destroyed an entire Roman legion. The Romans, who had not taken the battle very seriously, were shocked. Hadrian came in haste from the capital, and their greatest Roman general, Sextus Julius Severus, was called from Britain to command the expeditionary force.

Responding with ferocity, the Romans destroyed over nine hundred Jewish villages and fifty strongholds. By 135 the defending Jews were forced to retreat into a complex network of caves and tunnels, where they died or were starved out. Akiba, then in his eighties, was flayed alive, and Bar Kokhba was killed, probably in battle. Hundreds of thousands of Jews were thrown into slavery; they were so many that the going price for a Jewish slave was the equivalent of what it cost to feed a horse for a day. The death penalty was imposed for circumcision. The Romans almost totally eradicated Jerusalem—changing the city's name to Aelia Capitolina (Jupiter's Capital), plowing it under (leaving only a portion of the western wall of the temple), and banning Jews from its precincts except on the ninth of Ab, the fast day marking the first temple's destruction in 586 B.C.E.

Before the Bar Kokhba War, Palestinian Jewry was, if not substantial, at least a presence; after 135 not even that could be said. Where there had been an estimated 1.3 million Jews in Judea before the revolt, there were now only about 700,000. The remainder had either emigrated to the diaspora, or died in war, or been sold as slaves. From here until the mid-twentieth century, the story of Judaism is primarily the story of the diaspora.

With the deaths of Bar Kokhba and Akiba also faded the hope of an imminent salvation by the messiah. Messianism was no longer a high priority. Henceforth Jews would hope for the reconstruction of the great commonwealths of biblical and Maccabean times, but, with the exception of a messianic movement in the seventeenth century, they would not stake their lives on that hope until the Zionist movement of the twentieth century. As it was said, "The redemption of Israel will come step by step."

Of necessity, the Jewish leaders reached an accommodation with the Roman empire. One rabbi, tired of rebellions and anarchy, would declare, "Pray for the welfare of the government, for were it not for fear of the government, a man would swallow his neighbor alive."[4] Their success at dealing with new and difficult conditions is reflected in the fact that of all the ancient peoples of the Middle East, they were the only one to survive into the twentieth century with their identity and culture intact.

2. THE TALMUD

The story of the Jews in the first seven centuries of the common era, wrote the nineteenth century historian Heinrich Graetz, is a "history of suffering and scholars."[5] We have just looked at some suffering, and will soon look at more; let us now learn about the scholars. These were the rabbis who assembled the great commentaries on the Torah known collectively as the Talmud.

Many Christians inaccurately believe that Judaism is based solely on the written documents of Hebrew scripture, and especially the Torah. Some Christians also believe that the Torah is an outdated document composed of dry, legalistic, wholly intellectual, "unspiritual" statutes about the mundane events of daily life. This attitude demands correction. By the second century C.E., when the church fathers were attacking Judaism as a "dead faith," Jews were developing a new meaning for the words "Torah," "law," and "teaching."

The traditional definition was that the Torah was the written document that included the first five books of the Hebrew scriptures. A newer definition developed by the rabbis was that the Torah also included a body of oral interpretation of the written Torah that came to be called the Talmud (an Aramaic word that means "learning").

Before we look more closely at the Talmud, our appreciation of the work of the rabbis will be enhanced if we make an effort to understand some fundamentals of Jewish theology, and how they differ from Christian theology. Many Christians have trouble with the connection between faith and worldly behavior that is made in the Torah and the Talmud, and thus are frequently tempted to describe the documents pejoratively as "legalistic" and "unspiritual," and the Jewish God as "distant." Real differences in basic views of reality and in theology lie behind this misunderstanding. Those differences must be addressed if dialogue is to move beyond a superficial level.

Traditional Christianity tends to be marked by a dualism derived from Greek philosophy that divides reality into two distinct realms. These are the higher, transcendent, divine realm of ultimate truth, and the lower, carnal, worldly realm of shadowy truth. The religious question posed by this dualistic conception of reality is, "How do humans relate with and encounter God in this lower realm?" Without an encounter, "God" is a meaningless abstraction. For Christians, the encounter comes through the second and third persons of the Trinity, i.e., through Jesus Christ and the Holy Spirit. Without them, God would be unbearably distant; for them, God is supportively imminent.

On the other hand, most Jews do not share with Christians either an antipathy to the world or a need to make God wholly near or wholly other. In traditional Judaism, reality is all one, and God is equally imminent and transcendent; as Jeremiah wrote: "Am I a God at hand, says the Lord, and not a God afar off? . . . Do I not fill heaven and earth?" (Jer 23:23–24). The answer to the first question is *both;* to the second, *yes.* The same answers are given in different terms in this rabbinic reminder: "Wherever in the Scripture you find the power of God mentioned, there too you will find mention of His humility."[6] Perhaps the rabbi was thinking of the two radically different ways in which God appears to Moses in the book of Exodus. First, God speaks from the awesome mystery of the burning bush (Ex 3). Later, God is right down at the human level: "Thus the Lord used to speak to Moses face to face, as a man speaks to his friend" (Ex 33:11). While the conviction that God is both distant and near may seem paradoxical to the modern western mind, whose priorities are so firmly set on distinctions, the idea makes perfect sense to the mind that makes the basic religious assumption that God can do and be everything.

Widespread in Jewish theology is the idea that God has different attributes that are expressions of a single personality. These attributes are generally identified as creator, redeemer, and sustainer. The first attribute, the creator, is in the book of Genesis as well as in the ongoing creation celebrated on the sabbath. The second attribute, the redeemer, is seen in the liberating stories of the covenant and the exodus, as well as in the acknowledgment of human free will that is clear in God's gift of the ten commandments (for behind every law lies the assumption that people are free to choose to follow it). And the third attribute, the sustainer, is present in God's indwelling presence (called the shekinah) that suffers and rejoices with people in the daily events of life.[7] Rabbi Leon Klenicki gets at the second two attributes when he writes:

> Jewish spirituality is a meeting, an encounter entailing two dimensions. One is the covenantal relationship God-Israel, the other its implementation in a daily actualization of the experience of God, His Call and Presence, in individual and community existence.[8]

Although God has distinct attributes known in different ways, God is *one.* If any words of scripture can be described as the very essence of Judaism, they are the words of the Shema (Deut 6:4–5):

> Hear, O Israel: The Lord our God is one Lord; and you shall love the Lord your God with all your heart, and with all your soul, and with all your might.

"I am the first and the last," God says. "Besides me there is no god" (Is 44:6).

Because of their total commitment to a single God with different attributes, many Jews consider the Christian idea of a God in three persons to be polytheistic. We see this in the Talmud in a commentary on Isaiah 44:6:

> R. Abbahu said: An earthly king has a father, a brother, or a son; with God it is not so. For God says, "I am the first, for I have no father; I am the last, for I have no brother; and there is no god beside me, for I have no son."[9]

Daniel Breslauer addresses these fundamental differences in this way:

> Historically, Jews and Christians have been divided on their understanding of God's attributes of Creator, Redeemer, Sustainer. They find in Christian claims of a Trinity just the "cutting off of the roots" which Judaism defines as heresy. Christians, on the other hand, often fail to realize that Jews do have access to a close, intimate relationship with God. Redemption is as much a divine reality for Jews as for Christians. God's indwelling presence is a fact of Jewish experience no less than of Christian religious life. A monotheistic view of God should not preclude the existence of various paths to a hidden unity of divinity. Jews and Christians may well agree that God's essential nature is unity. They may allow each other the privilege of diverging ways of symbolizing that unity in a world of diverse and varied experiences of divinity.[10]

Now let us move on to the Talmud.

The problem that the Jews of Palestine faced in about 140 C.E. was enormous: when the temple fell in 70, and now—after the Romans finished mopping up after the Bar Kokhba War—with the loss of any semblance of control over the homeland of their ancestors, where would Jews find their focus? The answer lies in a penitential hymn written many years later:

> Nought has been left us,
> Save only this, our Torah.[11]

For many years oral interpretations of the Torah grew in number, were memorized, and were handed down from father to son. In time, they came also to be written down in the enormous compendium called the Talmud. The Talmud is "the single most influential document in the history of Judaism," writes Professor Jacob Neusner of Brown University.[12] Orthodox and many Conservative Jews regard the Talmud as equal in importance to the written Torah itself, and some Reform Jews agree. In the Christian tradition, there is no exact equivalent to the Talmud. It is neither scripture like the gospels or Paul's letters, nor a work of theology like St. Augustine's *City of God,* nor a book of order like canon law. Perhaps the closest that we can come to it—yet we are still a long way from similitude—would be the debates of the church fathers in the great ecumenical councils.

The rabbis said that all of the Torah—oral as well as written—was divinely inspired and preceded the creation:

> God created the world by the Torah: the Torah was His handmaid and His tool by the aid of which He set bounds to the deep, assigned their functions to sun and moon, and formed all nature. Without the Torah the world falls. . . . The Torah is God's handmaid, whom Moses was saintly enough to receive.[13]

Moses, it was said, was the rabbi for the rabbis. He taught both the written Torah and the oral Torah that came to be compiled and known as the Talmud.

The Talmud, like the written Torah itself, serves as a guide to Jewish life and Halakah. The oral teaching is important, the rabbis believed, because it provides moral guidance concerning relatively small matters, in turn facilitating observation of the large commandments found in the written Torah. In the words of the Talmud, oral law made "a hedge around the Torah."[14] Even when its particular strictures are outdated, the Talmud remains valuable because it offers guidance in the ways of making decisions.

Besides serving as a guide to ethical living, the Talmud also serves as a model process by which one approaches God. As we have seen, in Judaism daily life is never divorced from God. "Christians need to realize that Judaism stresses deeds as means to faith, not as substitutes for it," writes Breslauer. "Salvation is made possible because God graciously gave a Torah in which opportunities for a faithful turning to God are numerous."[15]

One process through which Jews experience God is to engage in communal discussions of and debates about the meaning of the Torah. In these discussions, the scripture is subjected to a detailed verse-by-verse analysis and interpretation called midrash ("to examine"). The result is part exegesis, part sermon. The Talmud contains the transcripts of thousands of these debates, many of them on very minor issues. Here is how

Jacob Neusner describes the Talmud and its makers in his book *Introduction to the Talmud:*

> The Talmudic method consists in rigorous, abstract argument about fundamentally practical, mostly trivial matters, an argument thoroughly articulated and tested against all possible objections. The Talmudic inquiry is phrased as a singing conversation among open and rational minds, united by a devotion to reason and commitment to unobstructed criticism, and dedicated in common to the cause of applying reason to the mundane issues of the workaday world. . . . What I find strange and awesome is that the rabbis, unlike us, were able to conceive of practical and critical thinking as holy. They were able to claim sainthood in behalf of learned men, to see as religiously significant, indeed as sanctified, what the modern intellectual perceives as the very instrument of secularity: the capacity to think critically and to reason.[16]

Study then becomes an equivalent of prayer. No wonder, then, that the fathers of the Talmud are called "the sages."

The Talmud consists of three major parts. One is the Mishnah ("that which is to be learned by repetition"). It is a didactic discussion of a code of law based on the written Torah. There are six major divisions dealing with large topics—for example, family, sabbath, and sacrifices—and in addition a total of sixty-three tractates dealing with smaller topics within those divisions. This is the main body of Halakah—the teaching. The Mishnah was written in Hebrew under the direction of the patriarch, or leader of the Palestinian Jews, Yehuda Ha Nassi (Judah the Prince), who died in 217 C.E.

The second part is the Gemara ("completion"), written in Aramaic, the daily language of the Middle East. This is a commentary on the Mishnah written as a narrative of debates between rabbis. The foundation of the Gemara is the Tosefta ("supplement"). The third part is the Talmud (the word also used to describe the entire collection). This is a commentary, also in Hebrew and in debate form, on the Mishnah and Gemara.

Although the word Talmud is normally used in the singular, there are two Talmuds. One is the Palestinian Talmud, written down in Palestine in the third through fifth centuries; the other is the Babylonian Talmud, written in Mesopotamia in the third through seventh centuries. It is called the Babylonian Talmud because the Jews of Mesopotamia were descended from the Jews who were exiled to Babylon in the sixth century

B.C.E. The Babylonian Talmud is three times longer and generally considered more authoritative than the Palestinian Talmud.

The oral interpretations were hammered out in long debates between the rabbis, for whom the arguments served as a combination of rallying cry and prayer. "Even though Israel be in exile among the nations," one rabbi said, "if they occupy themselves with Torah, it is as though they were not in exile."[17] Many documents show discussions taking place between several rabbis speaking for a particular interpretation or point of view. Often the participants actually lived years and even centuries apart; this indicates that the issues under discussion were more important than the disputants themselves. This ahistorical process should be familiar, at least in rough outline, to U.S. citizens who follow debates over constitutional law. There, the writings and speeches of the founding fathers of the eighteenth century, the opinions of distinguished jurists of the nineteenth century, and the intentions and decisions of lawmakers and judges of the twentieth century are all weighed and evaluated. It is as though James Madison, Chief Justices John Marshall and Earl Warren, and the current President and Speaker of the House of Representatives were in the same room.

The Talmud kept Judaism vibrant and contemporary by updating the Torah. With it, Halakah was clearly laid out for Jews desiring, as did their ancestors, to live a life that was sanctified and still part of the world. Asceticism and monastic retreat, so important to traditional Christianity, are not an option in Judaism, which seeks to find sanctification in daily life. Too, the Talmud brought the Torah to the people. "It was a durable Torah which these schoolmen had left behind them," writes Gedaliah Alon, "but it was accessible to everyman."[18]

The following long excerpt from the tractate on the sabbath in the Babylonian Talmud is a good example not only of how the rabbinic debates were conducted, but also of how flexible the rabbis were in shaping their interpretations of the Torah around the exigencies of contemporary life.

At issue here is what activities are permitted on the sabbath, the holy day of rest. As the argument develops, we learn much about the values of Jews living in Mesopotamia at the time the excerpt was written (probably about 320 C.E.). The Torah text for the debate is Exodus 20:8–10: "Remember the Sabbath day, to keep it holy. Six days shall you labor, and do all your work; but the seventh day is a Sabbath [rest day] to the Lord your God. . . ." The question is, in a busy community: What is "your work" and what is "God's work"?

R[abbi] Hisda and R. Hamnuna said that it is permissible to make plans for good deeds on the Sabbath; and R. Elazar said that one may arrange about alms to the poor on Sabbath. R. Johanan said: One may transact business which has to do with the saving of life or with public health on Sabbath, and one may go to synagogue to discuss public affairs on Sabbath. R. Jonathan said: One may even go to theaters and circuses on Sabbath for such a purpose. And in the school of Manasseh it was said that one may talk about the future marriage of one's children on Sabbath, or about the children's education, or about teaching them a handicraft, for the Scripture forbids "*thy* business," but "*God's* business" is permitted.[19]

This commentary summarizes a long-running debate; the speakers lived in a 150-year period between 219 and 375 C.E., and came from the diaspora as well as Palestine. It will help Christians put aside the old charges of "Jewish legalism" inspired by places in the New Testament where Jesus is criticized for healing on the sabbath—for example, Mark 2:23–3:6, John 5, and John 9. The obvious point here is that pursuits of health, community, family, and education are "God's work." This should not be surprising to anyone familiar both with Jewish respect for learning and with the tradition of Jewish mutual aid, which has played a significant part in Jewish survival over all the centuries of persecution. Another text from the same tractate reinforces the concern with education: "Let not the children be kept back from school, even to help in building of the Temple."[20]

In the Talmud, the rabbis worked to make the Torah a vital moral force. Here are a few examples, some direct and others almost poetic:

On persecution: "God loves the persecuted, and hates the persecutors."[21]

On human relations: "R[abbi] Hanina bar Dosa said: He in whom the spirit of his fellow-creatures takes delight, in him the Spirit of the All-present takes delight; and he in whom the spirit of his fellow-creatures takes not delight, in him the Spirit of the All-present takes not delight."[22]

On forgiveness: "Learn to receive suffering, and forgive those who insult you."[23]

On love: "All love which depends on something, if the thing ceases the love ceases. Love which does not depend on something never fails forever. What love is that which depends on something? That is the love of Amnon and Tamar [2 Samuel 13]. And that which does not depend on something? This is the love of David and Jonathan [1 Samuel 18]."[24]

On the sanctity of small acts: "A fire once broke out in Drokeret, but the neighborhood of R. Huna was spared. The people thought that it was due to the merit of R. Huna, but they were told in a dream that R. Huna's merits were too great, and the sparing of his neighborhood from fire too small a matter to attribute the marvel to him, and that it was due to the merits of a certain woman who used to heat her oven, and place it at the disposal of her neighbors."[25]

On the salvation of non-Jews: "There are righteous men among the nations [i.e., the Gentiles] who have a share of the world to come."[26]

And finally, *a reflection on humility* that echoes Jesus' saying about the first being last and the last being first (Mk 9:35): "Whoso makes great his name loses his name, and whoso adds not makes to cease, and he who does not learn deserves killing, and one who serves himself with the crown passes away."[27]

3. THE TALMUD AND THE SCRIPTURES

Besides serving as a guide to Jewish life, oral law was valuable because it was distinctively Jewish. Of course, that had been the case with the written Torah and the rest of Hebrew scripture, but when the Jewish Bible was translated into Greek and Christianity sprang up in the midst of Judaism, that claim of exclusivity no longer could be made. As Jews came to discover, Christians not only knew the written Torah of Hebrew scripture but also laid claim to it.

When the early Christians read the Jewish Bible, they did it not within the context of the Jewish tradition but in a way that read the Jewish story as a prediction of, or allegory for, the story of Jesus Christ. A Christian searches Hebrew scripture for texts that prove Jesus to be the fulfillment of Judaism. The approach is nicely summarized by St. Augustine: "In the Old Testament the New is concealed, in the New Testament the Old is revealed."[28]

One well-known example of this kind of reading is the way in which Christians have traditionally interpreted the collection of beautiful love poems known as the Song of Solomon (known also as the Song of Songs) as a hymn to the marriage of Jesus with the church. Another is the prophet Isaiah, especially the "suffering servant" song (Is 52:13–53:12), which, according to many Christians, was written solely as a prediction of Jesus' life and passion.

As another example, St. Justin Martyr (c. 100–165) saw Noah as a prefiguring of Christ. His argument shows this kind of reading in full flower:

For righteous Noah, along with the other mortals at the deluge, i.e. with his own wife, his three sons and their wives, being eight in number, were a symbol of the eighth day, wherein Christ appeared when He rose from the dead, for ever the first in power. For Christ, being the first-born of every creature, became again the chief of another race regenerated by himself through water, and faith, and wood, containing the mystery of the cross; even as Noah was saved by wood when he rode over the waters with his household.[29]

Allegorical exegesis would be acceptable if Jews were granted primary rights to the text's use and Christians only reserved the privilege to interpret it in their own way. However, that was rarely the case. Of Jewish predictions of Christ, Justin Martyr says that "David sang them, Isaiah preached them, Zechariah proclaimed them, and Moses wrote them." Justin then asks the Jew whom he is trying to convert, "Are you acquainted with them, Trypho? They are contained in your Scriptures, or rather *not yours, but ours.*"[30]

Not all the church fathers appropriated Hebrew scripture for their own ends. Some went entirely in the other direction to deny its legitimacy altogether. Marcion, a contemporary of Justin Martyr and a member of the Christian community in Rome, rejected the god of the Hebrews as a cruel tyrant totally other than, and subordinate to, the forgiving God of the Christians. Marcion energetically went about compiling a safely de-Judaized Christian scripture, censoring all quotes from and references to Jewish scripture from the writings that met with his approval (these books were Luke's gospel and ten of Paul's letters). In 144 C.E. Marcion was declared a heretic for sharing the two-deity theory of the Gnostics. It is not too much of an exaggeration to say that Marcionism lives today in every church whose order of worship does not include a passage from Hebrew scripture.

The early church sided with the kind of imperial exegesis practiced by Justin Martyr, and included most of Hebrew scripture in the official canon with Christian writings. To differentiate them, the Jewish writings were called the "old" testament (or revelation), as distinct from the "new" one.

That was the situation in the second century C.E. For Jews, what all this meant was that they no longer had an exclusive claim to the remarkable scriptures that had given them their identity as the chosen people of God. Therefore, to regain the privacy and autonomy that the Hebrew scriptures had granted before the coming of Christianity, the rabbis developed their unique oral commentaries on the written Torah. And as the following two commentaries make clear, they gave oral Torah the same status as the written Torah:

> God gave the Israelites the two Laws, the Written Law and the Oral Law. He gave them the Written Law with its 613 ordinances, to fill them [the Jews] with commandments, and to cause them to become virtuous, as it is said, "The Lord was pleased for His righteousness' sake to increase the Law and make it glorious." And He gave them the Oral Law to make them distinguished from the other nations [Gentiles]. It was not given in writing so that the nations should not falsify it, as they had done with the Written Law, and say that they are the true Israel. Therefore it says, "If I were to write for him the many things of my law, they would be counted as strange" [Hosea 8:12]. The many things are the Mishnah, which is larger than the [Written] Law, and God says, "If I were to write for Israel the 'many things,' they would be counted as strange [by the Gentiles]."[31]

> R. Judah, the son of R. Shalom, said: Moses desired that the Oral Law should be written also. But God foresaw that the Gentiles would one day translate the Torah and read it in Greek, and say, "They [the Jews] are not [the true] Israel." God said to Moses, "The nations [Gentiles] will say, 'We are [the true] Israel, we are the sons of God,' and Israel will say, 'We are the sons of God.' And now the scales are evenly balanced." So God said to the Gentiles, "Why do you claim to be my sons? I know only him who has my mystery in his possession; he is my son." Then the Gentiles ask, "What is thy mystery?" God replied, "It is the Mishnah."[32]

4. SIBLING RIVALRY

It may be helpful to attempt to find an analogy that will help Christians clarify the difficult relationship between two faiths that share so many characteristics and a common body of scripture. The most helpful analogy is that of another close relationship with which we are all familiar: that between siblings. Anybody who has been a brother or sister or who has parented brothers or sisters knows about the creative and destructive potential of sibling rivalry, with its violent swings between respect and contempt, love and hatred, security and competition. If brothers and sisters can be their most bitter enemies in times of jealousy, in times of reconciliation they can be their most loving friends.

This reality is frequently reflected in Hebrew scripture: Isaac and

Ishmael, Jacob and Esau, eleven of Jacob's sons and their brother Joseph —all were alienated from each other over the issue of who would receive their fathers' special favor, and then in various ways were reconciled either to their father or with each other (Gen 16, 25, 27, 33, 37, 43–45). In the gospel of Luke, Jesus echoes this theme in the parable of the prodigal son. The wastrel younger son returns home looking for money and prepared to confess his sins. Seeing him approach, his father rushes to him and kisses him before the son can get the words out of his mouth. Then, after the confession, the father has his servants prepare a feast in the prodigal's honor because "my son was dead and is alive again; he was lost and is found."

That is what most of us remember about the parable of the prodigal son. But there is more. The older brother, who has been working conscientiously in the fields, sees how his wayward brother has been welcomed by their father and (understandably) is angry. Once again the father comes to one of his sons, this time lovingly to soothe the older son's feelings of rejection: "Son, you are always with me," the father assures him. "and all that is mine is yours" (Lk 15:11–32).

There are thus two reconciliations in the story, each between a son and the father; clearly, once reconciled to their father, the sons will be reconciled to each other.

In her book on Christian antisemitism, *Faith and Fratricide,* Rosemary Ruether proposes that the parable of the prodigal son serve as a model for Christian-Jewish reconciliation. The younger brother is the Christian, whose expectation of the imminent second coming of Christ (the parousia) is disappointed. He returns home to his father (God)—not to give up Christianity, for the hope of the original vision will never die, but in repentance for his sins and seeking reconciliation. When the ever-faithful older brother (the Jew) sees the grand reception accorded the prodigal by the father, he feels rejected, but the father's reassurance brings peace and friendship. For Ruether, the key event is the return of the Christian wastrel—that is, the Christian return to eventual accommodation with the elder brother, Judaism.[33]

NOTES

1. Cf. E. Mary Smallwood, *The Jews under Roman Rule* (Leiden: Brill, 1976), p. 397.

2. *Ibid.,* p. 541.

3. *Ibid.,* pp. 434, 431.

4. Ab. Zar., 4a, in Claude G. Montefiore and H. Loewe, eds., *A Rabbinic Anthology* (New York: Schocken, 1974), p. 562.

5. Cf. Gedaliah Alon, *The Jews in Their Land in the Talmudic Age* (Jerusalem: Magnes, 1980), vol. I, p. 1.

6. Megillah, 31 a, in Montefiore and Loewe, *op. cit.,* p. 30.

7. Cf. S. Daniel Breslauer, "God: Jewish View," in Leon Klenicki and Geoffrey Wigoder, eds., *A Dictionary of the Jewish-Christian Dialogue* (New York/ Mahwah: Paulist Press, A Stimulus Book, 1984) pp. 73–76.

8. Leon Klenicki, "Exile and Return: Moments in the Jewish Pilgrimage to God," in Leon Klenicki and Gabe Huck, eds., *Spirituality and Prayer,* Jewish and Christian Understandings (New York/Mahwah: Paulist Press, A Stimulus Book, 1983), p. 1.

9. Exodus Rabbah, Yitro 29, 5, in Montefiore and Loewe, *op. cit.,* p. 12.

10. S. Daniel Breslauer, *op. cit.,* p. 76.

11. Cf. Gedaliah Alon, *op. cit.,* vol. I, p. 1.

12. Jacob Neusner, *Invitation to the Talmud* (New York: Harper, 1973), p. 65.

13. Tanhuma 1, f., 6b, in Montefiore and Loewe, *op. cit.,* p. 170.

14. Mishna Avot 1:1, in Clemens Thoma, *A Christian Theology of Judaism* (New York/Mahwah: Paulist Press, A Stimulus Book, 1980), p. 100.

15. S. Daniel Breslauer, "Salvation: Jewish View," in Klenicki and Wigoder, *op. cit.,* p. 182.

16. Jacob Neusner, *Introduction to the Talmud, op. cit.*

17. *Tanna de Be Eliyyahu,* 148, in C.G. Montefiore and H. Loewe, 132.

18. Gedaliah Alon, *The Jews in Their Land in the Talmudic Age,* vol. I, 22.

19. Babylonian Talmud, *Sabbath,* 150a, in C.G. Montefiore and H. Loewe, 193.

20. Babylonian Talmud, *Sabbath,* 119b, in C.G. Montefiore and H. Loewe, 520.

21. Mishnah, *Pesikta Rabbati,* 193b, in C.G. Montefiore and H. Loewe, 462.

22. *Aboth,* III, 13, in *ibid.,* 468.

23. Babylonian Talmud, *Abboth de Rabbi Nathan,* XLI, 67a, in C.G. Montefiore and H. Loewe, 462.

24. *Pirke Aboth,* V:19; R. Travers Herford, *The Ethics of the Talmud,* 138.

25. Babylonian Talmud, *Ta'anit,* 21b, in C.G. Montefiore and H. Loewe, 182.

26. *Tosefta,* Sanhedrin, XIII:2, *ibid.,* 604.

27. *Pirke Aboth,* I:13; R. Travers Herford, 33.

28. Augustine, *The Spirit and the Letter,* variously in chs. 18, 22, 30.

29. Justin Martyr, *Dialogue with Trypho,* ch. 138.

30. Emphasis added. *ibid.,* Chapter 29.

31. *Numbers Rabbah,* Naso, XIV, 10, in C.G. Montefiore and H. Loewe, 159.

32. *Pesahim Rabbah,* 14b, in *ibid.,* 161.

33. See Rosemary Ruether, *Faith and Fratricide* (New York: Seabury, 1974), 254–257.

III. The Heritage of Hate

In the early 1960s a survey of Christian attitudes about Jews found that thirty-nine percent of Protestant and Catholic church members "at least considered it possible that the suffering of modern Jews actually stemmed from divine will" as a consequence of their and their ancestors' rejection of Jesus. Forty-two percent of Episcopalians surveyed said that Jews were most responsible for the crucifixion.[1]

If these startling statistics tell us anything, it is that history does not go away. All too often, we uncritically pray the prayers, think the thoughts, and speak the words of our forebears, no matter how ill-considered and even cruel those prayers, thoughts, and words may be. Therefore the importance of the first few centuries of Christianity must not be underestimated. According to the Roman Catholic educator Gabriel Moran, "Western culture cannot continue unless it heals the split that occurred in the first century of the common era."[2]

The challenge for Christians today is to become conscious of the longevity of that early split—in all its violent rhetoric and often violent behavior—and to find ways to heal it without losing the distinctive nature of what it means to be a Christian. The Jewish-Christian dialogue, then, is at least partly a *monologue,* a self-examination by Christians that eventually will lead not only to healthier relations between the followers of the two faiths but also to a better understanding of what it means to be either a Christian or a Jew. The path is not easy, but it must be undertaken.

This is why Jewish-Christian dialogue must inevitably include some discussion of the foundational years of Christianity in the first through fourth centuries, when the church fathers established the theology and rhetoric of the new faith and its attitude toward its elder sibling. In this chapter we will look at some of those tales and teachings which provided the motivation for the anti-Judaic laws discussed later.

42

1. THE RHETORIC OF CONTEMPT

As we saw in Chapter I, self-examination was a necessary fact of life for any first century Jew who became a follower of Jesus. The first great Christian theologian, St. Paul himself, was sorting out his own religious identity in his letters to the scattered churches of the Roman empire. We see Paul at his most introspective in his letter to the Romans, where the apostle addressed the ambiguous situation in which the chosen people of God, the Jews, were joined by the Gentiles under God's dispensation. Consistent with his belief that God's grace excludes nobody (see Gal 3:28), Paul, in Romans 11, clearly believes in the continuing significance of Judaism: "I ask, then, has God rejected his people? By no means!" (Rom 11:1). In this light, Judaism and Christianity continue on parallel tracks.

However, this decisive affirmation was compromised as soon as it was made by Paul's and his followers' rejection of the Jewish law (with circumcision and dietary laws) as signs of the covenant for gentiles. In saying this, Paul and his followers made it equally clear that for Gentiles, Jewish *practice* was outdated because Jews did not follow the dispensation of grace. Here, the two faiths are not parallel. There is a single track, on which Christianity has priority over Judaism. Of these two convictions— the first showing the two faiths coequal, and the second showing Christianity dominant—the one that came to prevail in Christianity was the second. And so began the great tradition of contempt for the Jews.

The language that the early Christians used in their attack on Jews took several forms that have long survived their originators. The most enduring terminology was a contrast between a higher, "spiritual" Christian approach and a debased, "carnal" Jewish approach. One of the earliest examples is the way in which Justin Martyr (c. 100–165) unfavorably contrasted the "carnal" fleshly circumcision of the law with the "spiritual" and "true" circumcision of Christ, and the "physical" Israel of Hebrew scripture with the "spiritual" Israel of Christ and the New Testament. "The Jews," Justin said, "are a people hard-hearted and without understanding, both blind and lame, children in whom is no faith."[3]

That was tame compared with the ultimate and most long-lived attack. Hanging everywhere was the tradition of Jewish corporate responsibility for the death of Jesus. The four gospel accounts vary in detail but they agree that at least some Jews brought Jesus up before the Roman procurator, Pontius Pilate, on capital charges.

Exactly what those charges were has been a subject of considerable dispute for a very long time. The scholar E.P. Sanders has plausibly argued that in the eyes of the high priests and the Romans, Jesus' major crime was a combination of offenses: first, he gathered a group of followers; and, second, he attacked ("cleansed") the temple, the very center of Jewish spiritual life, and predicted its destruction (Mt 21:12–13; Mk 11:15–19; Lk 19:45–48; Jn 2:13–17).[4] For the Romans, who reserved the sole power to execute criminals, all this smacked of disorder in a community whose potential for nationalistic rebellion was well-known, as we saw before. That Jesus was from Galilee, that hotbed of revolt, must have prejudiced Pilate, who was notorious for chasing down and executing Galilean nationalists. Therefore it is extremely likely that, to quote Paul Winter's scholarly study *On the Trial of Jesus,* "Jesus was arrested, accused, condemned, and executed, on a charge of rebellion."[5]

Now how many Jews should be held responsible for pressing charges? The authors of the synoptic gospels give extremely qualified answers to that question. Mark says that as soon as the Pharisees encountered Jesus for the first time, they "held counsel with the Herodians, how to destroy him" (Mk 3:6). Matthew says that "the chief priests and the whole council sought false testimony against Jesus, that they might put him to death" (Mt 26:59). In Luke "the chief priests and the rulers and the people" cried "Crucify, crucify him" (Lk 23:13, 21). That is to say that not "all Jews" but only certain parts of the Jewish community took action against Jesus. But the tradition memorialized throughout the history of the church, and honored in the Good Friday liturgy, has no such careful qualifications: Pilate "went out to *the Jews,*" announced Jesus' innocence, and asked for his release, but *the Jews* shouted, "Not this man, but Barabbas!" (Jn 18:38–40; emphasis added).

These issues reached a whole new level of significance as the church fathers struggled to come to an understanding of the nature of Jesus. As a consensus began to form that Jesus was the divine Son of God, the charges against the Jews became extremely grave. Scapegoating and demonizing of *all Jews* as deicides (God-killers) appeared early in those crucial formative years in the first and second centuries and was regularly echoed in the legends and myths that were created by the early believers, as well as in the writings and sermons of the church fathers who put together the theology and church structure that we have inherited.

2. THE MAKING OF MYTHS

No movement will thrive and grow without a few heroes who are held up as role models to pass on values, identify goals, and encourage followers in times of despair. Sometimes these heroes live and triumph, but often they die as martyrs to their faith or country. In either case, their stories typically are passed on in a highly romanticized form that bears little semblance to the original, simple account.

In the early church, the martyrologies—the accounts of the deaths of the saints—were valuable documents, as important to Christians as the stories of soldiers killed in battle are to people on the home front during a war. In both cases, the martyr defends purity against evil; the difference is that while the martyred soldier is killed in the act of attacking the enemy, the Christian hero dies passively, just as Jesus died. As a reward for her or his witness, the martyr goes on to eternal life to serve as an ambassador for God from humans.

While the martyrologies helped build Christianity by keeping alive the spirit of the foundational crucifixion stories, they did so at a price. In mirroring the dramatic passion accounts of the gospels, they also mirrored (and often enhanced) the latent and explicit anti-Judaic elements in the Christian tradition. Heroes must have enemies, and the most obvious enemies were the people whom, it was said, Jesus came to save but who rejected and killed him.

James W. Parkes, an Anglican priest who perhaps more than any other Christian deserves to be called the father of Jewish-Christian dialogue, collected many of these martyrdom legends in his book *The Conflict of the Church and the Synagogue,* published in 1934. Here is a sample of these stories, some of which are notable for their fancifulness and contradictions:

> Joseph of Arimathea [see Mark 15:43] was immured by the Jews in prison, and left to die of starvation. He is found, in perfect health, forty years later by Titus on the capture of Jerusalem. Alternatively, he is released by Christ Himself, and continues preaching.

> Mary, the mother of Jesus, was much persecuted by Annas and Caiaphas [the high priests, see Luke 3:2] but when they tried to burn down her house, they were themselves burnt. At the Ascension, the Jews tried to stone her, but they killed fifty of each other instead.

> Thaddeus [another name for the faithful apostle Judas], after suffering many torments from Gentiles, or Jews and Gentiles, died in peace. Alternatively, he is martyred in Persia.

> Mary Magdalen suffered many outrages from the Jews, but finally died in peace. Alternatively, she followed St. John to Ephesus, and was buried outside the cave of the seven sleepers.[6]

Even more indicative than these tales is the development of a legend that is not in Parkes' collection—the story of the martyrdom of St. James, the brother of Jesus and the president of the church in Jerusalem. He is sometimes called James the Less or James the Just in order to distinguish him from the disciple of the same name. The Christian scriptures present him as a very human man of the world who originally doubts his brother's sanity but eventually becomes the leader of the Jerusalem church (see Mk 3:21, 31–35; Jn 7:5; Acts 15:13–21, 1 Cor 15:7). However, the church's tradition portrays him in a very different way. Even the use of the word "brother" to describe him in the Christian scriptures (Mt 13:55; Mk 6:3; Gal 1:19) was subject to mythmaking. Some church fathers of the second through fourth centuries, believing that a fraternal relationship compromised Mary's virginity, decided that he must have been Jesus' stepbrother —a son of Joseph from a prior marriage. For St. Jerome (c. 347–420), even that was not enough. To protect Mary's virginity and so further heighten the purity of Jesus' birth, Jerome concluded that they were merely cousins.

What is best known about James is his martyrdom in Jerusalem in 62 or 63 C.E. The story was told by two writers with very different goals in mind. One account is a straightforward narrative written in about 90 C.E. by the Jewish historian Josephus Flavius, and the other is a martyrology produced a century later by Hegesippus, a Jew who converted to Christianity.

According to Josephus, the new high priest Ananus hauled James and some of his colleagues before the sanhedrin (the Jewish ruling body) on charges of having violated the law. A Sadducee, Ananus was noted for a hot temper and judicial severity. James was found guilty and stoned to death at a place and in a way that Josephus does not describe. We know that this action was illegal because by Roman law the Roman procurator had to approve all meetings of the sanhedrin as well as all death sentences (see Jn 18:31), and the newly appointed procurator Albinus was on his way to Palestine from Rome. Ananus' actions offended Jews whom Josephus describes as being "the most reasonable of the citizens and strict observers of the law" (meaning, most likely, the Pharisees). They protested to King Herod Agrippa II, who fired Ananus as high priest after only three months. But it was too late to save James, the victim of a power play by an ambitious, opportunistic official.

Hegesippus' narrative is more exciting and gory. His goal throughout seems to be to show that James was the victim of a widespread Jewish anti-Christian conspiracy. He holds accountable not the high priest but the entire Jewish community, which he pejoratively describes as "a tumult of the Jews and the scribes and Pharisees." He tells us that at Passover, this mob forcibly placed James on the highest part of the ramparts of the second temple and demanded that he persuade Christians (described as "straying after Jesus who was crucified") to change their ways. In response, Hegesippus tell us, James converted many onlookers in a speech predicting that Jesus "will come on the clouds of heaven." James' successful preaching only angered the Jews, who mocked him by his nickname "the Just," and then heaved him from the wall:

> So they went up and threw down the Just, and they said to one another, "Let us stone James the Just," and they began to stone him since the fall had not killed him, but he turned and knelt saying, "I beseech thee, O Lord, God and Father, forgive them, for they know not what they do."[7]

It seems that the Jews' killing frenzy was so great that even a sympathetic Jewish priest pleaded for mercy, pointing out that James was praying for his persecutors. His efforts were unavailing, and a fuller (a laundryman) put James out of his misery with the club used to beat clothes. The body was buried on the spot, at the foot of the temple wall.

Where Josephus emphasizes a division among the Jewish establishment and its Roman rulers, in which James plays an incidental role, Hegesippus tells a much more elaborate story whose central figure throughout is the apostle. In his choice of words and events, Hegesippus persistently conjurs up images of the gospel crucifixion scenes. In both martyrdoms the persecutors are Jewish mobs running wild without Roman complicity, the persecutors mock the victims, and the martyrs convert onlookers, find sympathy in a supposed enemy, and pray for the forgiveness of their murderers (using almost exactly the same words; see Lk 23:13).

Josephus wrote an historical account. Hegesippus, however, wrote an inspiring faith story. He worked hard to draw parallels with the passion story and made no effort whatsoever to provide factual information that might get in the way of his story's theme. This information would have included the legal limitations on Jews in the Roman empire, the leadership role played by the sanhedrin and the high priest, and Jewish purity laws that make burial at the temple wall highly improbable. As if those contradictions were not enough, there is other evidence that Hegesippus' story is fanciful. For example, he portrays James not as the busy administrator of the Christian scripture accounts but as an ascetic who spent his days praying in the temple "so that his knees grew hard like a camel's because of his constant worship of God."

Which account did the church choose as the official one? The answer is the same as the answer to the following questions: In which account are the early Christians put in the best light and their enemies in the worst? In which are the difficult ambiguities of Jewish-Christian relations most quickly glossed over? In which are there simple heroes to praise and simple villains to despise? In short, which story best serves the needs of a struggling movement rather than the dictates of accuracy?

The answer is obvious. When the first church historian, Eusebius (c. 263–339), got to the martyrdom of James in his *Ecclesiastical History,* he repeated Hegesippus' story because, he wrote, it "gives the most accurate account." Ever since, the official Christian story of the martyrdom of St. James the Just, whose saint's day is October 23, has been an echo of the crucifixion and a fulmination against the Jews. His symbol in the church's iconography tells all: it is not a bishop's chair or a symbol of justice but, rather, a Jewish fuller's club.

3. THE CHURCH AGAINST THE JEWS

The central purpose of Hegesippus, Eusebius, and their successors was to uplift the Christian message, not to malign Jews. But one of their main strategies in doing this was to develop the argument that the strength of Christianity is best represented by the debasement of the people who reject it. Eusebius opened his history with a declaration that his purpose was "to recount the misfortunes which immediately came upon the whole Jewish nation as consequence for their plots against our Savior."[8]

The early efforts at building the new faith through invented, highly romanticized accounts of the lives and deaths of early Christian martyrs had two important side effects. First, they clearly identified collective Judaism—all Jews and not an individual priest, and not Herod or Pilate —as the enemy who killed Christ and Christ's witnesses. Second, these legends allowed Christians to persecute Jews or, at the least, to explain away Jewish suffering under persecution as justified punishment by God. For example, Justin Martyr, in his *Dialogue with Trypho,* has his Christian speaker explain to a Jew why he has suffered so much after the Bar

Kohkba revolt. The reason, Justin says, has nothing directly to do with the revolt. "These things have happened to you in fairness and justice, for you have slain the Just One, and his prophets before him; and now you reject those who hope in him, and in him who sent him—God the almighty and maker of all things—cursing in your synagogues those that believe in Christ."[9]

Similar attacks appeared in the mouths of some of the church's most respected theologians. A widespread tactic was to take out of context the many criticisms by Jews of other Jews that are found in the Jewish Bible. For example, in Exodus 32 when Moses attacks the idolatry of the golden calf he is not saying that all Jews at all time are idolators. This limitation, however, was not always mentioned by Christians writing against Jews.

The attacks increased in number and intensity after Christianity became the official imperial religion subsequent to the ascension of Constantine in 312. For example, St. Ambrose, the bishop of Milan (c. 340–397), who played a major role in establishing the church in Italy, incited his congregation to burn down a synagogue when he described it as "a house of impiety, a receptacle of folly, which God himself has condemned."[10] When the emperor objected, the synagogue was rebuilt.

Ambrose was not alone, and the emperors were not always so tolerant. Anti-Judaic diatribes appear to have been a staple of sermons in those days when the church was struggling with a variety of opponents in order to guarantee its position as the state religion. No doubt Christians also remembered with bitterness the days when Judaism was tolerated and Christianity was persecuted, sometimes with the help of Jews. The most vicious attacks appeared in a series of sermons given by one of the brightest luminaries of the early church, St. John, bishop of Antioch (c. 347–407). If we are to believe his nickname, *Chrysostom,* which means "Golden-Mouthed," John was a remarkable preacher, certainly a passionate one. Between 387 and 389, his eight homilies against the Jews were aimed mainly at keeping Christians out of the synagogues of Antioch, the major city in the eastern Mediterranean and the site of the first churches founded outside Jerusalem. His vitriolic homilies betray a shaky confidence about the church's success. One after another, John repeats a litany of diatribes: the synagogue is "worse than a brothel . . . the den of scoundrels . . . the temple of demons . . . the cavern of devils"; Jews are assassins of the Son of God; their punishment, while seeming to come from their fellow humans, is from God, who has withdrawn their inheritance "because he hated you, and rejected you once for all. . . ." His defense of persecutions was blatant: "So whenever the Jew tells you: It was men who made war on us, it was men who plotted against us, say to him: Men would certainly not have made war unless God permitted them."[11]

4. AUGUSTINE AND THE ROLE OF JEWS

Compared with Ambrose and Chrysostom, St. Augustine, bishop of Hippo in North Africa (354–430) and one of the most influential theologians in the history of Christianity, was relatively favorable to Jews. Perhaps Augustine's mild judgment was conditioned by a different environment, for unlike Milan and Antioch, in Hippo the most dangerous challengers to orthodox Christianity were not Jews but Christian heretics. But there were also strong theological reasons why Augustine did not altogether reject Jews. Augustine was greatly influenced by Paul, and, like Paul in the letter to the Romans, he could not simply dismiss the ancient scriptures, the covenant, and the Jews themselves, all of which he believed played a large role in God's plan.

However, the place that Augustine found for the Jews was hardly one of equality with Christians. Among the descriptions that he used to describe the Jews were "unwilling witnesses" to Christianity's truth, "stationary in useless antiquity," and "slaves" under Christian mastery.[12] Further, he believed that the Jews have denied the clear evidence of their own scripture, and their continuing woes offer permanent instructions about the price of rejecting Jesus. In addition, he urged Christians to work for their conversion: "Let us preach to the Jews, whenever we can," he wrote. "It is not for us to boast over them as branches broken off. . . . We shall be able to say to them without exulting over them—though we exult in God—'Come, let us walk in the light of the Lord.' "[13] But with all these qualifications, Augustine differed from many of the other early Christian writers in calling for a secure, protected place for Judaism. That was much more than a Chrysostom would allow.

Augustine's theology of toleration of the Jews was grounded on two convictions that echoed Paul. First, the Jews have brought the scriptures to the Christians; second, their conversion to Christianity will herald the second coming.

The issue concerning the scriptures was important. Like most early Christians, Augustine engaged in the allegorical exegesis that saw Hebrew scripture as a Christian document. For example, he read an invitation to convert to Christianity into Isaiah 2:5, "O house of Jacob, come let us walk in the light of the Lord." He had plenty of precedent for this kind of exegesis going back to the Christian scriptures themselves. In the book of

Acts, Peter—apparently referring to Psalm 16:10—says that King David "foresaw and spoke of the resurrection of the Christ" (Acts 2:31). Paul himself provided the general rule of thumb for reading the Jewish scriptures as Christian prophecy when he told the Corinthians: "He was raised on the third day in accordance with the scriptures" (1 Cor 15:4). These words were repeated in the Nicene Creed.

For Augustine as well as for Paul, it was vital to prove that the Jews had long predicted that the divine spirit and power would assume flesh in Jesus. These predictions proved the pre-existence of the divine Logos (or Word) that became embodied in Jesus Christ. They were also Christianity's best argument in the effort to convert pagans. Augustine's term for the Jewish people, "slave librarians," indicates his attitude. In ancient Rome, the slave librarian was a well-educated slave who served as tutor to a family's children. As Augustine used the term, the first word referred to the Jews' status under Christians, and the second word, "librarian," reflected the educational service of retaining the scriptures. For this librarianship, they are not to be killed but rather dispersed "in order to bear this testimony, so that the church of Christ has everywhere increased." To use a biblical analogy, Jews are the elder brother, like Cain (Gen 4:15), who must be allowed to live in order to serve the younger brother, Christianity.[14]

Augustine's second argument for toleration was that Jewish resistance to Christ was part of God's plan. Paul had written that their conversion would bring salvation to the world, but had not explained exactly why this would be the case (Rom 11:11-15). Augustine provided the reasoning. The conversion of the Jews was a key step in an elaborate timetable that Augustine constructed for the final judgment and the end of time:

> And at or in connection with that judgment the following events shall come to pass, as we have learned: Elijah the Tishbite shall come; the Jews shall believe; Anti-Christ shall persecute; Christ shall judge; the dead shall rise; the good and the wicked shall be separated; the world shall be burned and renewed. All these things, we believe, shall come to pass, but how or in what order, human understanding cannot directly teach us, but only the experience of the events themselves. My opinion, however, is that they will happen in the order in which I have related them.[15]

While Augustine's theological arguments for the toleration of Jews seems patronizing and controlling from our perspective, its importance must not be underestimated, for, as we will see, it served as the Jews' lifeline for hundreds of years.

5. ANTI-JEWISH LEGISLATION

Myths shape popular opinion, and popular opinion affects laws. Before Constantine, the Roman empire's laws concerning Jews were, on the whole, relatively benevolent in comparison with its laws concerning Christians, whom pagans scorned as unpatriotic atheists. But the tables were turned after Christianity became the official faith of the empire in the fourth century C.E. Of the two extremes in Christian theological thinking about Jews—the hatred of people like John Chrysostom and the qualified tolerance of Augustine—the legal status of the Jews tended to reflect the more tolerant attitude until the eleventh century, when the crusades brought an entirely new aspect to the relations between Jews and Christians.

The goal of much of the empire's legislation, inspired by the church, seems to have been not so much to persecute Jews as to separate Jews and Christians who, to the consternation of the church, joined together not only in social relations but also in worship in both synagogues and churches. The widest chasm between social customs and the church's wishes was in Spain, where Jews had been prominent for many years, and where they were regarded legally as citizens of the empire.[16]

The church tried to change all that in 306 at its Council of Elvira, in Spain. The Spanish bishops prohibited Christians from, first, intermarrying and having sexual intercourse with Jews unless the Jewish partner was converted; second, exchanging hospitality with unconverted Jews; and third, having rabbis bless their fields. Obviously Christians and Jews had developed a relationship of exceptional intimacy if they regularly intermarried, dined in each other's houses, and relied on each other for spiritual assistance. All of this was too much for the Spanish bishops, who certainly must have held Augustine's opinion that the relationship should be that of masters to slaves rather than friend to friend. In the words of the Jewish historians Max L. Margolis and Alexander Marx, "At this early period there came to light the double picture characteristic of Spanish Christianity at all times, gross worldliness among the laity and fanatical severity among the higher clergy."[17]

After the rise of the emperor Constantine in 312 many similar regulations aimed at leveraging Christians away from Jews and the synagogue were legislated by church councils and then adapted as official imperial policy. At first only a handful of laws directly or indirectly affected Jews' rights to worship as they pleased. One of these was a law written in 383 requiring for the first time that rabbis perform certain public duties before being permitted to fulfill their religious obligations.

In 438 all current laws were unified in the Theodosian Code (named for the emperors Theodosius I and II). Under the code, Judaism continued to be a *religio licta,* with its own clergy, holy days, and houses of worship protected from mob attack. However, there were some indirect proscriptions that profoundly affected Jewish freedoms. While it was illegal to disturb or damage a synagogue, Jews had to have official permission before a synagogue could be repaired. Synagogues, unlike churches, were not regarded as places of legal asylum. Proselytism, which the pagan empire had banned because it stirred up trouble, became legal for Christians but was banned entirely for Jews; the fact that this law was necessary suggests that Jews competed rather successfully with Christians for converts. Although Jewish families were prohibited from disinheriting converts to Christianity, converts to Judaism became intestate. The legal status of Jews was also circumscribed: they could not give legal testimony against Christians, nor were they allowed to enter the army and assume some official positions (including the job of jail warden, apparently because most prisoners were Christians). Other laws limited Jewish property rights: Jews were prohibited from owning slaves who were Christians and from circumcising (that is, converting) slaves who were pagans. The tax burden on Jews was disproportionately heavy.

To combat Judaizing trends in Christianity, some laws dealt with liturgy and the calendar. At the Council of Nicea in 325 the western bishops came up with a system of determining the date of Easter so that the holy day would not fall during Passover (following the fourth gospel). Christians were prohibited from the Passover seder; likewise, Jews were banned from Easter services. One council required Christians to read from a gospel as well as from Hebrew scripture during worship; this suggests that some Christians looked to the Jewish Bible for their inspiration. In 425 the empire destroyed any remaining semblance of Jewish nationalism by dissolving the institution of the patriarch, who for more than three hundred years had ruled the Jewish community in Palestine.

In these years there developed a pattern that would hold sway for centuries: the Jews' best friend was the emperor, who did what he could to protect them from mob rule. Sometimes this favor was entirely misleading. For example, the emperor Julian who was called "the Apostate" because he rejected Christianity in favor of paganism during his brief two year reign (361–363) promised to return Jerusalem to Jewish rule in exchange for Jewish support for his invasion of Persia. Some construction began in Jerusalem during the Jewish reoccupation (the first since 135 C.E.), but Julian was killed during the war, and soon the city was back in Roman hands.

Some popes, too, protected Jews. Citing Paul, Pope Gregory the Great (540–604) assiduously defended the rights granted Jews under the Theodosian Code—for example, ordering the reconstruction of synagogues destroyed by Christian mobs and opposing forced baptisms of Jews. Yet with equal energy he observed the code's restrictions and encouraged ever-stronger efforts at conversion.

By the eighth century the Theodosian Code had lost its influence in the expanding cities of western Europe, where Jews were becoming as important as citizens and tradespeople as Spanish Jews had been. For instance, in Lyons, France, market day was shifted from Saturday to another day to allow Jews to shop and sell, and some Jews had Christian servants. In those relatively tolerant days, the fulminations of John Chrysostom against an immoral people pretty much faded away, and if the average Christian accused Jews of any sin it was the obvious one of lack of faith in Jesus Christ, and even that was of modest consequence. The Carolingian kings defended the Jews in their realm against the attacks of the church, which followed the Augustinian theology of toleration only in life-and-death matters. Charlemagne (768–814) appointed an official called *magister Judaeorum* ("master of the Jews") to protect Jews from attacks by the clergy, and his son Louis the Pious (814–840) declared apostolic backing to "follow divine mercy and make no distinction between faithful and infidel."[18] Jews were now permitted to testify against Christians in court (it is of interest to note that at times three Christian witnesses were considered to have the legal authority of between four and nine Jewish witnesses). Jews were even allowed to prevent their slaves from being baptized by Christians.

While these improvements were welcome, by no means did they end anti-Jewish sermons and occasional popular uprisings against Jews. St. Agobard, the archbishop of Lyons (778–840), fought a nasty and on the whole unsuccessful campaign against imperial toleration. One of the major influences on later antisemites, Agobard once argued in a letter to another bishop that Jews are

> cursed in the city and cursed in the country, cursed in their coming in and their going out. Cursed is the fruits of their loins, of their lands, of

their flocks; cursed their cellars, their granaries, their shops, their food, and the crumbs of their tables.[19]

As it turned out, this reminder of the old hard days of Chrysostom was a hint of even worse things to come.

NOTES

1. Charles Y. Glock and Rodney Stark, *Christian Beliefs and Anti-Semitism* (New York: Harper, 1965) pp. 60–64, 195–197.

2. Gabriel Moran, "Endtime in Christian-Jewish Relations," in Timothy McCarthy, ed., *A Time to Live* (Romeoville: Christian Brothers Conferences, 1981) p. 25.

3. Justin Martyr, *Dialogue with Trypho,* in *The Ante-Nicene Fathers,* A. Cleveland Coxe, ed. (Grand Rapids: Eerdmans, 1981), vol. I, chaps. 16, 18, 11.

4. E.P. Sanders, *Jesus and Judaism* (Philadelphia: Fortress, 1985), p. 304.

5. Paul Winter, *On the Trial of Jesus* (Berlin: DeGruyter, 1974²), p. 69.

6. James Parkes, *The Conflict of the Church and the Synagogue: A Study in the Origins of Antisemitism* (New York: Hermon, 1974), pp. 402–404.

7. Cf. Eusebius, *The Ecclesiastical History* (New York: Putnam, 1926), book II, chap. 23.

8. *Ibid.,* book I, chap. 1.

9. Justin Martyr, *op. cit.,* chap. 16.

10. St. Ambrose, quoted in Malcolm Hay, *The Roots of Christian Anti-Semitism* (New York: Freedom Library/ADL, 1981), p. 25.

11. John Chrysostom, quoted in Edward H. Flannery, *The Anguish of the Jews* (New York/Mahwah: Paulist Press, A Stimulus Book, 1985²), pp. 50–52; and in Malcolm Hay, *op. cit.,* pp. 26–32.

12. Cf. Alan T. Davies, *Anti-Semitism and the Christian Mind: The Crisis of Confidence after Auschwitz* (New York: Herder & Herder, 1969), p. 64.

13. St. Augustine, quoted in Edward H. Flannery, *op. cit.,* p. 53.

14. St. Augustine, *The City of God* (Garden City: Doubleday/Image, 1985), book XVIII, chaps. 46–47.

15. *Ibid.,* book XX, chap. 30.

16. Jews called Spain, the place of this successful exile, "Sephard" (see Ob 20). The Jews who were expelled from Spain in 1492 were known as "Sephardic Jews."

17. Max L. Margolis and Alexander Marx, *A History of the Jewish People* (New York: Temple/Atheneum, 1972), p. 304.

18. Cf. Edward H. Flannery, *op. cit.,* p. 83.

19. Malcolm Hay, *op. cit.,* p. 34.

IV. Further Stages of Conflict in Europe

Christians eager to help eradicate the pestilence of antisemitism face a paradox: much of the culture of anti-Judaism and antisemitism is deeply rooted in values and ideas that lie at the very foundations of Christianity. We have seen how some of those ideas developed in early Christianity. Now we will look at how people relied on them to justify horrific persecutions of Jews.

The assumption lying behind the traditional Christian understanding of the role of Jews in God's order developed primarily from ideas gleaned from St. Paul and St. Augustine: that Jews play a vital role in God's scheme for salvation because of what they contribute to Christians and Christianity. The logic of this theology goes as follows:

(1) The great event in history, Christians believe, is the coming, death, and resurrection of the Son of God. This event not only turned Judaism into a "dead" faith, but it was accurately predicted in the Jewish scriptures. Jews who do not convert to Christianity misread the true "spiritual" significance of their own scriptures and fully deserve every punishment that God has imposed on them, often through the agency of the church.

(2) Yet, according to this theology, Jews still serve two important divine purposes. First, they are the "book-bearers"—the means by which the scriptures reach Christians. Christianity depends on Hebrew scripture, for without the "old" testament there can be no "new" testament. Second, the Jews' resistance to conversion heralds the future arrival of the end-time, of the second coming. It was projected that soon after the Jews will convert, Jesus will reappear.

(3) Therefore, this logic concludes, because of the essential role that Jews play in God's scheme, their survival must be tolerated.

For the past two thousand years, most Christians have interpreted "toleration" to mean "toleration in debasement." Christians have allowed Jews to suffer the exclusions and degradations that, according to the church fathers, God has ordained to be their inevitable and just due. Here is how the monk Peter of Blois expressed this conclusion in the twelfth century:

> Even today the Jews are to be allowed to live, because they are our enslaved book-bearers, as they carry around the prophets and the law of Moses for the assertion of our faith. Not only in their books but also in their faces do we read of the passion of Christ.

Happily, some modern theologians are challenging the assumption that Judaism is important only insofar as it aids the church triumphant. The key element is appreciating the possibility that God can act in the world in more than one way. The German theologian Franz Mussner writes: "The Church must finally see that alongside itself there is still another supernatural element in the world in which God is present and works in the world: the Jewish people."[1] The U.S. theologian Rosemary Ruether makes the same point:

> The supersessionary pattern of Christian faith distorts both Jewish and Christian reality. We should think rather of Judaism and Christianity as parallel paths, flowing from common memories in Hebrew Scripture, which are then reformulated into separate ways that lead two peoples to formulate the dialectic of past and future through different historical experiences.[2]

And the authors of an article in a recent textbook on Christian theology claim: "Faith in Jesus Christ is not a substitute for Israel's faith but a new universal availability of divine presence."[3]

Despite its clear limitations, the traditional Christian theology of Judaism had one positive outgrowth: Since the church believed that the Jews play a key role in Christian salvation, it could not countenance their physical elimination. The result was that, at least in principle and frequently in fact as well, the church hierarchy became the protector of the Jews, even if that protection came at a price of severe limitations of freedoms.

Yet not all Christians were absolutely pure in their regard for this theology, which had to compete with other, more hostile traditions. Among these traditions were: all Jews are responsible for the death of Jesus Christ; a Christian's responsibility is to convert Jews; the only alternative to a converted Jew is a dead Jew; Jews must not be permitted to assimilate themselves into Christian society. The tension between these convictions and the dominant theology of toleration in debasement was deep, and the results were unpredictable.

1. THE CHALLENGE TO "TOLERATION"

The Augustinian theology received its most severe challenge in the period 1100–1400, partly because of intellectual shifts and partly due to social pressures. In order better to understand Jewish scripture, some Christians learned Hebrew, and a few engaged rabbis in deep and even friendly dialogue whose goal, rather than conversion, was mutual understanding. Inevitably these Christians came across the Talmud and contemporary commentaries. One of the commentators was the Spanish-born philosopher Moses Maimonides (1135–1204), who wrote a version of the Mishnah for laypeople as well as the masterpiece *The Guide of the Perplexed,* and whose mastery of the ideas of Aristotle greatly influenced St. Thomas Aquinas and other Christian scholastic theologians. In reading contemporary Jewish authors, Christians finally came to realize, one thousand years after the rabbis began to collate the Talmud, that Judaism was far from "stationary in useless antiquity," as Augustine once said.

The discovery of a living Judaism unsettled many Christians. If Judaism was dynamic, then what did that say about the church, which for centuries had been defining itself in opposition to a "stagnant," "dead" Judaism? One solution to this problem is to accept the challenge and reevaluate Christianity—a methodology chosen by an increasing number of Christians today. But when this challenge first appeared seven hundred years ago, the church chose to counter-attack. In 1239 Pope Gregory IX declared the Talmud to be heretical; three years later, copies of the Talmud were publicly burned in Paris under papal instructions. While at this distance it may seem absurd that any Christian could feel qualified to call a Jewish document heretical, that is in fact what happened. Christians had so thoroughly appropriated the Hebrew scriptures as their own that a pope could without embarrassment torch a Jewish commentary on those scriptures, much the way he would destroy a manuscript written by a misguided Christian. The conviction that all truth could be unified in a single, authoritative belief would allow no other response to this challenge. This was the beginning of the decline of the theology of "toleration."

2. THE CRUSADES

At about the same time that the pope burned the Talmud, local, popular persecutions of Jews began to take place in western Europe. Which event triggered the other, or whether they occurred simultaneously, is debated by historians. But such questions pale before the violence that began in the 1090s and scarcely slowed for the next six hundred years, first under the Roman Catholic Church and later under both Catholics and Protestants.

The eleventh century was the turning point. Before then, reasons given by Christians for persecuting Jews fell into three general categories: first, as collective punishment for something that "they" once did, i.e. the murder of God; second, as punishment for something that "they" refused to do, i.e. convert to Christianity; third, to separate "them" from Christians. In the late eleventh century and thereafter, Christians who harassed or killed Jews continued to cite these reasons, but they also added another: Jews are to be persecuted for the deviltry that they do *now*. Here, truly, is the acting out of the demonization of the Jews of John 8:44: "You are of your father the devil, and your will is to do your father's desires. He was a murderer from the beginning. . . ."

The starting point for the uprisings was an event that is much celebrated in the history of Christianity—the first crusade in 1096. This first mass Christian revival took the form of a military expedition to Palestine to attempt to win Jerusalem back from the Moslems, who had seized the city in 637. The main stimulus for the first crusade was the news of the destruction of the Church of the Holy Sepulchre, built over Christ's tomb. Pope Urban II urged the crusade with the words "*Deus volt*" (God wills it). The first crusade succeeded, and Jerusalem was conquered in 1099, only to be lost back to Islam in 1187. By 1272 a number of other crusades had been undertaken, most of them with the aim of retaking Jerusalem, but Palestine remained under Moslem rule until 1917.

The issue concerning Jews was not Jerusalem, where few Jews lived. Rather, the issue was the massacres of Jews that preceded and paralleled the first crusade and many of its successors. The chronicle of Richard of Poitiers starkly describes the crusaders' early activities:

> . . . before journeying to these places, they exterminated by many massacres the Jews of almost all Gaul, with the exception of those who accepted conversion. They said in effect that it was unjust to permit enemies of Christ to remain alive in their own country, when they had taken up arms to drive out the infidels abroad.[4]

Some Christians, eager to be counted among the ranks of the crusade to prove their faith but for one reason or another unable to journey to Palestine, expressed their religious passion by attacking their perceived enemies at home.

In the last years of the eleventh century, anti-Jewish hostility verging on mob rule swept many of the cities of France, England, and Germany. The death toll was great. It was said that at Mainz some nine hundred Jews either committed suicide with attackers at the door or were later slaughtered, and that in nearby towns more than one thousand men, women, and children died. At Worms, on May 25, 1096, crusaders and the mob following them killed an estimated eight hundred Jews who would not submit to baptism, some while singing psalms, and one while reading the Talmud. Several thousand died at Prague. And on across the map. Not everybody was a persecutor, and there were protests by powerful Christians. The holy Roman emperor and many lords and bishops protected Jews, and the emperor Henry IV allowed Jews to recant baptismal vows made under force. The church rethought the question of the validity of forced baptisms and in a papal bull of 1201 announced the doctrine that any baptism was illegal if the baptized person protested. Unfortunately, this law was academic, for those Jews who refused to accept baptism, as was usually the case, were immediately murdered.

Around the time of the first crusade the image of the Jew in Christian eyes began to become malevolent. In one of his miracle poems, Gautier de Coincy described Jews as "More bestial than naked beasts/Are all Jews, without a doubt." In another poem, a Jewish child who converts to Christianity suddenly becomes beautiful, trustworthy, and amiable:

> Wiser still and much lovelier
> Than all the other Jews . . .
> To Christian children he looked full fair
> And played with them both "before and behind"
> Without the Jew, they knew not what to do.[5]

Hatred for Jews took form in two new manifestations that sprang up in the thirteenth century and lasted for centuries thereafter. The first was the persistent story that, at Passover, Jews engaged in ritual murders of Christian children and then mixed their blood with the unleavened bread eaten at the Passover meal. In some of the tales, the "murderers" also profaned the eucharistic host in some way. A common element in many of these rumors was that they were started by recent converts from Judaism to Christianity who, in their eagerness to win the approval of their new companions, invented elaborate anti-Christian "conspiracies" by Jewish elders.

The historian of antisemitism Leon Poliakov sees this ghastly rumor springing up in the mid-twelfth century almost simultaneously in England, Germany, and France, and then sweeping through Europe. So widely did the fantastic stories spread that in a bull in 1247 Pope Innocent IV gave a summary lesson in Jewish law, pointing out that Jews are not allowed to touch a dead body at Passover. He protested the idea that "Whenever a corpse is found somewhere, it is to the Jews that the murder is quickly imputed."[6] The effect of these cautions was minimal.

These accusations justified the second of the two new manifestations, which was that Jews be singled out in appearance. As we have already seen, since the fourth century Christian leaders had been attempting to separate laypeople from Jews by banning social and religious intercourse. Apparently those regulations failed, for at the Fourth Lateran Council of 1215 the church took the unprecedented step of requiring Jews to wear distinctive dress. The temperament of the makers of this law is suggested by the fact that Moslems, heretics, lepers, and prostitutes were later added to the list. In some cities the Jews were required to wear special conical hats, but the insignia generally consisted of a large round badge (called the *roulle*); some were red or white, many were yellow. Sometimes Jewish merchants had to display the *roulle* outside their shops. Eventually urban Jews were forced to live together in a special district, which might be walled in and locked up at night. The name for this district, *ghetto,* may be derived from the Italian word *geto* ("iron foundry") because the first Jewish district, in Venice, was located near a foundry.

Symbolizing the Jews' uncertain status in western Europe was the controversial nature of one of the few trades permitted to them, that of usurer or lender of money at interest. Jews came to money-lending and banking not out of free choice but because they were banned from most other ways of making a living, including owning land and working in the trades. In the twelfth century, Christians were normally prohibited from lending money at interest, an act that many theologians considered to be a violation of natural law. Jews, who up until then had tended to specialize in commerce, were licensed to perform this necessary service. Although the Torah prohibits lending money at interest (for example, Deut 23:20 and Lev 25:35–37), the Talmud and medieval rabbis allowed it under the general context that basic justice in civil and business obligations required that the lender be compensated.

While some Jewish money-lenders became wealthy, it was a tenuous and often unprofitable living. The state took a large share of the interest in taxes, and powerful debtors frequently escaped their obligations by exiling or even killing the lenders. The kings often claimed the estates of Jewish lenders so that debtors would be beholden to them. Some anti-Jewish persecutions may have been motivated by a desire to avoid paying off debts. In any case, the Jewish monopoly on money-lending was short-lived, and by the end of the thirteenth century Christians were controlling the money markets.

3. THE JEWS OF ENGLAND

An excellent case study of the vagaries of Jewish history—of the rule of law countered by the rule of mob—is the story of the Jews in medieval England. Jews came to England from France in 1066 at the invitation of William the Conqueror, and at first they were treated fairly, although they were not allowed to own land or join guilds of artisans. Many were merchants and financiers, some of whom were extremely wealthy. But this did not shield them from persecution, either from the kings or at the hands of mobs. In 1144 in Norwich, Jews were accused of murdering a boy named William, and though the case was quickly dismissed, the boy was popularly regarded as a martyr, and the Jews of Norwich were persecuted for this incident. The English kings protected the Jews from the popular disturbances that surrounded the crusades, even as they heavily taxed Jewish wealth. Of the 130,000 pounds raised in the country for the third crusade, just under half was levied on the small minority of English Jews. King Henry II later imposed a property tax amounting to twenty-five percent on Jews.

At the coronation of Richard I in 1189, a mob attacked a delegation of Jewish merchants bearing gifts for the king, and many prominent Jews were murdered in the ensuing day-long riot, which ended only when the king proclaimed his protection. However, once Richard sailed off on a crusade, the riots began again. The worst was at York in 1190. The Jews sought protection in the royal castle where, besieged by a mob led by a monk and the county sheriff, who happened to be in debt to Jewish money-lenders, as many as five hundred either committed suicide or were slaughtered. The mob's next step was to raid the cathedral in search of debt records, which they promptly destroyed. On his return, Richard imposed high taxes on the Jews, which his successors continued to raise and brutally enforce. In 1210, when Abraham of Bristol refused to pay,

King John had one of his teeth extracted daily. After seven days, Abraham paid up.

Anti-Jewish events accelerated in England. In 1218 Henry III required Jews to wear the badge. Four years later the archbishop of Canterbury forbade them to mix with Christians or to build synagogues. In 1230 the personal property tax on Jews was raised to thirty-three percent. In 1253 Jews were prohibited from employing Christian servants, from eating or buying meat during Lent, from intervening in a fellow Jew's conversion to Christianity, and even from worshiping in a voice loud enough to be heard by Christians. In 1255 Henry III ceded to his brother his rights to tax English Jews, which in effect mortgaged the whole community. In the same year a Jew in Lincoln was forced to confess the murder of a boy named Hugh, whose body was found in a well, and eighteen Jews were executed over the objections of local Dominican monks. Geoffrey Chaucer memorialized Hugh's "murder" and the retribution in "The Prioress' Tale":

> O cursed folk of Herodes al newe! . . .
> O yonge Hugh of Lyncoln, slayn also
> With cursed Jewes. . . .

In 1275 Edward I took away one of the Jews' few economic opportunities by prohibiting them from lending money at interest—which was fairly academic since few Jews had any money to lend. In 1279 almost three hundred Jews were executed for debasing coins. A law passed in 1280 required Jews to listen to Christian sermons. And, finally, in 1290 Edward became the first western ruler to ban Jews from a nation when he ordered the Jews of England expelled on less than four months' notice. Sixteen thousand Jews took ship, leaving their few remaining residences and fortunes to be fought over by the Christians. Jews were not again permitted to live in England until 1656, more than one hundred years after the first publication of *The Book of Common Prayer.*

4. TO THE INQUISITION

A characteristic of virulent of anti-Judaism and antisemitism is that they frequently surface in mass movements. When the autocratic power of the state or the church was called into play concerning Jews, the purpose was not to attack them but rather to defend them from popular uprisings. This does not mean that the church and other authorities were exempt from blame for antisemitic acts. On the contrary, the mob was often influenced by theological anti-Judaism and even led by clergy; for example, the widespread persecutions of the late eleventh century followed directly on the church's historic interpretation that Jesus was killed by "the Jews," and were triggered by the church's crusade against non-believers in Palestine. The subtleties of St. Augustine's theology of "toleration" could easily be forgotten in moments of heat, when all that was remembered was that the Jews were thought to be "God-killers."

Weakened during the crusades, the church's theologically based policy for defending Jews began to be even less effective in the fourteenth century when church officials were hard-pressed by mobs hunting down scapegoats for the bubonic plague that killed off one-third of Europe. It was commonly believed throughout Europe that the devil—the antichrist himself—lay behind the black death, and that Jewish witches had been his agents, contaminating wells with poisons said to be made up of spiders, frogs, the communion host, and the hearts of Christians.

One reason for the latest conspiracy theory was the fact that Jews suffered relatively little from the plague. This was due in part to their enforced separation from Christians but more so to their observance of biblical laws of ritual purity, some of the very laws that Christians had been condemning since the time of St. Paul. The Torah's purity laws (Lev 11–15) require that people who come into contact with bodily discharges, skin eruptions, and corpses are to be regarded as unclean for set periods of time and until they wash themselves and their clothing. Written some twenty-five hundred years before scientists developed the theory of germs, these ritual laws provided good protection against many diseases.

The plague was not the only issue. There is considerable evidence that the root causes of the dreadful conspiracy theories included economic as well as health concerns. Forced into commerce and money-lending, the Jews became unofficial arms of the nobility, the state, the church, and Christian financiers. This made Jews easy targets of protest by the bourgeoisie and tradesmen, who believed that to eliminate the Jews was to eliminate their debts. They were mistaken, for the ruling class often took over the debts of the Jewish money-lenders who were killed.

Long after the plague faded into history, the demonization of Jews that surrounded it became attached to stereotypes of malicious money-grubbers like the usurer Shylock, Shakespeare's "Merchant of Venice," who demanded a pound of his debtor's flesh. To arguments that Shylock was an honest portrayal of one of Shakespeare's contemporaries we must reply that at no time during the playwright's lifetime—in fact, at no time in the two hundred and seventy-four years before his birth in 1564 and the forty years after his death in 1616—were Jews allowed to enter or live in England. The portrayal and its images in popular Christian mythology are based on stereotypes.

5. THE SITUATION IN THE REST OF EUROPE

At this time in Germany and France, a sustained popular effort to exterminate all Jews did away with national and even regional laws that protected them, leaving them at the whim of local nobles who, if they invited Jews to settle, set a price of taxation that could more accurately be called extortion. Local churches did not always resist; for instance, of the four expulsions from Mainz between 1420 and 1471, three were directed by the town's archbishop.

The rapid end of the relative toleration of antiquity and the middle ages came as a shock to Jews. After centuries of being treated as permanent, productive residents of the towns and cities of Europe, they quickly became people having (according to a French legal document in 1361) "neither nation nor territory of their own in all of Christendom where they may remain, frequent, or reside."[7] This fortified the legend of the "wandering Jew." Whenever the Jews were permitted to settle down, they were allowed only the back streets of the big cities. At times they were even walled in in the ghetto. Yet for all their crowding and discomforts, the ghettos were places where Jews could live in self-sufficiency and, as we have just seen, in relatively good health apart from Christians. A language unique to these communities was developed: Yiddish, which is medieval German flavored by Hebrew and some eastern European languages and written in Hebrew letters, right to left. The name "Yiddish" is derived from *Yid Deutsch,* or *Jüdische Deutsch*—"Jewish German." Until quite recently, Yiddish was the language of many European Jewish immigrants to the United States.

Eastern Europe became a haven for Jews fleeing, first, the crusaders and, later, the mobs. In Poland, the Jewish population more than tripled to fifty thousand between 1500 and 1648. This was the "golden age" of eastern European Jewry: a Jewish parliament was accountable only to a tolerant king, Jews were chosen to manage the estates of the Polish nobility, and Jewish education thrived. But this golden era, like so many others in Jewish history, was blown apart when the Cossacks, mercenary soldiers originally brought together from Greek Orthodox communities to fight the invading Tatars, rose up against the Polish Catholic aristocracy and their Jewish retainers. On June 10, 1648, Cossacks led by Bogdan Chmielnicki killed six thousand Jews at Nemirov, Poland, and over the next decade they slaughtered thousands more and destroyed about seven hundred Jewish towns and settlements. The descendants of the few remaining Jews lived in the "Pale of Settlement." These were the provinces that were seized by Russia in the eighteenth century.

Alongside these physical abuses, the legal attacks on Jews multiplied. Their oaths were not accepted in court, and they were prohibited from attending universities. A tradition linking Jews with witchcraft developed in connection with the plague and also out of the ancient charges of deicide and blood-libels. Rumors spread about Jewish doctors: Charlemagne allegedly had been killed by one, and, according to no less an authority than the Vienna Faculty of Medicine, Jewish physicians were required to do away with every tenth patient.[8] These tales did not stop several popes from relying on Jewish doctors, but of course that was not commonly known. Jews were pilloried as God-killers in passion mystery plays, portrayed with the devil's horns in cathedral statuary, and hunted down, sometimes as witches, sometimes as ritual murderers, and at other times as potential converts, by St. Vincent Ferrer and other Dominican friars who served as the soldiers of the bloody inquisition.

A major goal of the inquisition was to convert Jews, but even conversion did not solve a Jew's problems. In Spain, once the home of another "golden age" of Judaism, a series of persecutions and bloody riots led many Jews to convert. Hated by Jews who rejected baptism, and distrusted by Christians as show-converts who secretly observed Jewish practices, which for many was the case, these apostates were contemptuously called *Marranos* ("swine"). In 1478, the pope authorized Queen Isabella to establish the Spanish inquisition to hunt down a widely perceived Marrano "plot" to recant baptismal vows. Between February and November 1481, almost three hundred Marranos were burned at the stake in the *auto da fé* ("act of faith"). Even the bones of dead Marranos were dug up and burned. Using trumped-up charges of ritual murders and secret cabals, the inquisitor general, Torquemada, fanatically hunted down carriers of Jewish blood, which, given the historic tolerance of Spain, flowed through the veins of even royalty and bishops.

The last service that Jews provided for Spain was to pay a special tax to finance Isabella's war against Granada, the remaining Moslem state in Iberia. Granada was taken on November 1491. On March 30, 1492, the one hundred and fifty thousand unconverted Jews of Spain were given three months' notice to leave the country. Called *Sephardim,* these heirs of the great Jewish communities of Spain fled to North Africa, the Middle East, northern Europe, Brazil, and, eventually, England and North America. Six Jews sailed with Christopher Columbus, who used navigation tables written by a Jewish astronomer named Abraham Ben Samuel Zacuto. Sephardic Jews made up the first Jewish community in the western hemisphere, in the Dutch settlement of Recife, Brazil. The term Sephardic now applies generally to Jews who are not from central Europe, the latter being referred to as the *Ashkenazim.*

6. JEWISH MYSTICISM

Partly in defense against these depredations and partly in reaction to highly intellectualistic trends in Jewish life, several mystical movements sprang up in many Jewish communities in the twelfth century and after.

Despite the crude Christian attacks on Judaism as being "non-spiritual" and "legalistic," a non-intellectual, mystical element had long existed in Judaism. While mysteries abound in Hebrew scripture—think of the burning bush (Ex 3)—the most vivid example in the Jewish Bible is in the book of Exekiel. The prophet's vision of the great winged chariot and his repeated phrase, "wherever the spirit would go, they went" (Ez 1), are hardly the product of a dry, soul-less faith.

A different form of mysticism later appeared in the books of the Hebrew Bible that scholars call "wisdom literature"—the books of Job, Proverbs, Daniel, and the Wisdom of Solomon. There the writers lovingly described a personified force called Wisdom who mediates between God and humans. Job asks, "But where shall Wisdom be found? And where is the place of understanding? Man does not know the way to it, and it is not found in the land of the living" (Job 28:12–13). Job's question is answered in the Wisdom of Solomon, where Wisdom is referred to as a woman and is described as "a breath of the power of God, and a pure emanation of the glory of the Almighty" (Wis 7:25).

This Jewish wisdom tradition may have been influenced by Greek ideas introduced into Israel after Alexander the Great conquered the Middle East in 325 B.C.E. Of particular importance was Plato's dualistic theory that ultimate reality lies in non-worldly "forms" or "ideals," which our temporal surroundings only reflect. Some scholars believe that the idea of personified wisdom emanating from God is an important source of the Christian "Logos theology" set forth in the first three verses of John's gospel, and of the Nicene Creed's statement that the Son of God is "eternally begotten of the Father."

But the great flowering of mysticism began in the twelfth century with the teachings called the *Cabbala* (also *Kabbala*), in which human beings come into union with God in mysterious ways, and in which not only religious acts but all human actions have their own mystical aspect. In this melding of philosophy, the esoteric, and Jewish tradition, the precepts of the Torah were taken most seriously. Of the Cabbala, Abraham Joshua Heschel, the great student of Jewish mysticism, wrote:

> A new form of living was the consequence of the Cabbala. Everything was so replete with symbolic significance as to make it the heart of the spiritual universe. How carefully must all be approached. A moral rigorism that hardly leaves any room for waste or respite resulted in making the Cabbalist more meticulous in studying and fulfilling the precepts of the Torah, in refining his moral conduct, in endowing everyday actions with solemn significance. For man represents God in this world. Even the parts of the body signify Divine mysteries.[9]

The goal of the Cabbalist is different from that of the Christian mystic, whose aim is to purify the body and mind through ascetic practices. As Heschel put it: "The purpose of man's service is to 'give strength to God,' not to attain one's own individual perfection. Man is able to stir the supernal spheres."[10]

Besides the secretive followers of the Cabbala, the great mystics of Judaism have been and continue to be the *Hasids,* the "pious ones." We first encountered the *Hasids* back in the first chapter; they were the forerunners of the Pharisees. The term reappeared in Germany in the period 1150–1250, when a group of Jews—called *Haside Ashkenaz* ("the Devout of Germany")—and led by Rabbi Judah ben Samuel of Regensburg—developed a mystical, ascetical approach to the Torah. Their approach is summarized as follows in their major treatise, *Sfer Hasidim* ("The Book of the Pious"):

> All your actions should be for the sake of heaven. Let a man not eat or sleep with the intention of being healthy and fattened in order to engage in matters of this world and to pursue wealth. He should rather say, "I will sleep and I will eat in order that I may be able to stand in fear of my Creator and engage in His Law and commandments."[11]

A third group of Hasids appeared in eighteenth century Poland, and their descendants still thrive today. This Hasidism was founded on the ruins of a disastrous Jewish messianic movement that began in 1648, the year of the terrible Cossack rebellion in Poland. It was also the year that Cabbalists predicted would be the one which would see the appearance of the messiah. A young Turkish Cabbalist named Sabbatai Zevi indicated that he was the messiah. Over the next twenty years he traveled around the eastern shore of the Mediterranean, gaining an almost universal following among Jews. The word spread to Europe, where Jews hungry for liberation sold their belongings so as to be unencumbered when the call came to return to the holy land. In synagogues everywhere, prayers were said for "our Lord and King, the holy and righteous Sabbatai Zevi, the Anointed of the God of Jacob."[12] The self-proclaimed messiah was, if anything, a confident leader. He ordered the Jewish calendar altered to account for his long-awaited arrival. For example, the Ninth of Ab, for centuries the day on which Jews mourned the destruction of the temple, now became a day of rejoicing because it was his birthday. Declaring 1666 to be the year of restoration, he boldly sailed to Constantinople where, he was sure, Sultan Mohammed IV would bow before him.

The sultan, however, threw him into prison. To prove his messiahship, Sabbatai Zevi summoned witnesses, one of whom, a Polish prophet named Nehemiah Cohen, denounced him as a fraud and a revolutionary. When he was called before the sultan, the putative messiah put on a turban and, changing his name to Mehemet Effendi, converted to Islam. Since he promised to bring converts after him, the sultan protected Mehemet/Sabbatai until somebody caught him chanting the psalms in Hebrew, when he was exiled to a village in Albania where he died in 1676. Such was the strength of messianism and mysticism, so powerful were the hopes of the Jews, that many believed that Sabbatai Zevi had neither converted nor died, and a movement in his name continued for seventy-five years.

In Poland, the Jews who had survived the Cossacks were now doubly distressed because they had seen their hopes for the messiah shattered. The rabbis attempted to reconstruct Jewish culture along traditional scholarly lines, with schools and written commentaries on the Torah and Talmud. In protest against this intellectual approach there appeared a pietistic, emotional reaction centering on a village called Medzebozh, in the Polish state of Podolia on the Turkish border. The leader was a mystic named Israel (1700–1760), who came to be known as the *Baal Shem Tov* ("Master of the Good Name"), abbreviated as the *Besht*. The Besht was no scholar. A synagogue sexton's helper, with a limited education and little skill at interpreting the Torah and Talmud, he lived his faith in an intense prayer life that was interspersed with exuberant dancing. The

Besht's message was simple: the best way to come into unity with God, who is everywhere and near, is not in focused study but in joyful prayer and worship. In this way, even the most common, unlearned person can reach God. Many of the marvelous stories that grew out of the Besht's movement are told by Elie Wiesel in *Souls on Fire* and *Four Hasidic Masters.*

So disruptive did this new Judaism seem to rabbis who had devoted their whole lives to the study of the Talmud that the Hasids, as the Besht's followers were inevitably called, were excommunicated in 1772. The movement faltered but survived in various groups defined by their villages and the families of their charismatic leaders, called *Tzaddikim* ("righteous ones," "saints"). When Hasids had the opportunity to emigrate from eastern Europe in the 1930s and 1940s, they rejected the message of Zionism. Israel, they believed, would be formed by the messiah, not by the hands of men and women. Thus they settled in the United States.

To say that the Hasids are to mainstream Judaism what the Amish are to mainstream Christianity would be an exaggeration, for, unlike the Amish, the Hasids use such products of modern technology as automobiles and refrigerators. Yet the spirit of community, separateness, and uncompromising anti-secularism is similar in both movements. In his best-sellers *The Chosen* and *The Promise,* novelist Chaim Potok not only opens a window to this type of Judaism, which otherwise is unknown by most Americans, but he also portrays some of the tensions that exist between two major approaches to Judaism: on the one hand, the ultra-Orthodox, those mystically-minded Hasids who place their hopes in the future coming of the messiah and resist the temptation to assimilate with modern secular life, and, on the other hand, less rigid, more worldly, Zionist Jews who, all the same, are observant of the Torah.

In a moving section in *The Chosen,* which is set in the United States in the 1940s, Potok gets to the heart of the differences between the two approaches in a moving description of two reactions to the terrible announcement of the details of the holocaust. One reaction is that of the Hasidic *Tzaddik* Rabbi Saunders; the other is that of the non-Hasidic Orthodox Jewish scholar David Malter, a Zionist working actively for the establishment of a Jewish state in Israel. The story is told by David Malter's son Reuven:

> "The world kills us," Rabbi Saunders says when he hears the grim news. "Ah, how the world kills us. . . . How the world drinks our blood. . . .

How the world makes us suffer. It is the will of God. We must accept the will of God."

He then asks God, "Master of the universe, how do you permit such a thing to happen?"

When Reuven tells his father about Rabbi Saunders' question, David Malter asks if God responded. "Reb Saunders said it was God's will," Reuven answers. "We have to accept God's will, he said."

"You are satisfied with that answer, Reuven?" his father asks bitterly.

"No."

"I am not satisfied with it either, Reuven. We cannot wait for God. If there is an answer, we must make it ourselves."[13]

7. THE PROTESTANTS

The Protestant reformation of the sixteenth and seventeenth centuries did not bring about much, if any, improvement in Christian attitudes about Judaism. Many of the events of the twelfth and thirteenth centuries were repeated in the sixteenth. The fact that both were periods of intense religious renewal cannot be coincidental. Just as antisemitism seems to run with mass uprisings against the states and princes that protect minorities, the contagion also appears to be a predictable element in revivals of faith, in which true believers reduce subtle issues of spirituality and history to simplistic creeds, wild slogans, and immoderate ideological allegations.

While the main issue of the reformation was the criticism by some Christians of other Christians, the theological debates also reflected and affected Christian attitudes about Jews. Some Protestants came out of the reformation with a healthier respect for Judaism. The Protestant emphasis on scripture led many to a more open-minded attitude about the Jewish Bible and Jews in general. Meanwhile, many Protestants (for example, the Puritans) felt a special affinity for Jews as they wandered from country to country in their own diaspora.

Still, many grounds of contention remained. The most basic issue was the old one: the vast majority of Jews continued to "reject" the gospel and refused to convert to Christianity. In addition, there were fundamental theological differences between the two faiths that became entangled in the reformers' critique of orthodox Catholicism, which they saw as heretically reliant on "works." In their attacks on Rome, reformers were repeatedly drawn to analogical interpretations of the New Testament critiques of the "legalistic Jews" who stubbornly refused to understand that salvation came by grace alone. "The letter killeth, but the spirit gives life" (2 Cor 3:6), Paul's epigrammatic criticism of Torah observance, was borrowed by the reformers to attack Rome much the same way that early Christians appropriated the prophets of the Hebrew Bible to attack Jews. Indulgences and other requirements by the medieval church were deemed inherently "Jewish" in their legalism. For example, the seminal Swiss reformer John Calvin (1509–1564)—who was not antisemitic to the degree that Martin Luther was—wrote that he had abolished many of the Roman church's ceremonies "partly because by their multitude they had degenerated into a kind of Judaism, partly because they had filled the minds of the people with superstition."[14]

If there was something "Jewish" about non-dependence on God's grace, then there was also something "Jewish" about the reformers' opponents, whatever their background. Some reformers bunched together Jews, Turks, Papists, and heretics as people who did not believe in the doctrine of justification by faith alone. Anti-Judaism, in short, received new legitimization when the traditional anti-Jewish polemic became the language of Christian reform.

Obviously, that there were and remain major differences between Christianity and Judaism must be acknowledged by anybody attempting to engage in dialogue. On the one hand, many Christians emphasize the importance of salvation by God's initiative (grace) over salvation by one's own good behavior (works or law). They say that only God can take the initiative; if a Christian behaves ethically and does good works, that is a sign that she or he has been saved; it is not the cause of salvation. On the other hand, many Jews neither stress salvation nor arbitrarily distinguish between grace and law. The Jewish emphasis is nicely expressed in the Talmudic saying, "Better is one hour of repentance and good works in this world than all the life of the world to come."[15]

S. Daniel Breslauer carefully distinguishes the two approaches as follows:

> Christians need to realize that Judaism stresses deeds as means to faith, not as substitutes for it. Salvation is made possible because God graciously gave a Torah in which opportunities for a faithful turning to God are numerous. The Jew does not earn salvation by applying large quantities of sterile actions. Only one action, faithfully performed, is sufficient. God's grace, however, has made the faithful turning possible through the instrument of Torah.[16]

This idea would have been scorned by the most influential of Protestant reformers, Martin Luther (1483–1546). Of the epistle of James, the one works-oriented letter in the New Testament, Luther wrote that it was "full of straw because it contains nothing evangelical,"[17] and deleted it from his canon of accepted books.

Yet as sharp as this theological criticism is, it does not explain why late in his life Luther unleashed a torrent of hateful anti-Jewish sermons and letters that to this day embarrass Lutherans, if not all Protestants. In his 1543 tract, "On the Jews and Their Lies," he urged the burning of synagogues and Jewish homes, the seizing of prayer books and Talmuds, the banning of teaching by rabbis, and the end of safe-conduct passes for Jews. In his final sermon, preached three days before his death in 1546, he declared the end of toleration: "If they turn from their blasphemies, we must gladly forgive them; but if not, we must not suffer them to remain."[18]

Luther spoke in an anti-Jewish polemic partly because his culture was anti-Jewish. For example, in 1519 (during Lent, when Jew-baiting by Christians was particularly prevalent), all the Jews were expelled on only four days' notice from Regensburg, one of the largest and oldest ghettos in Germany and the center of the Hasidic movement of the twelfth century. The instigation appears to have been a local uprising by Christian peasants against all authority, including (to quote a contemporary writer) the "idle, lecherous, and greedy" Jews.[19] In 1519 the bishop of Speyer said of Jews, "They are not human beings but dogs."[20]

The bitter edge of Luther's polemic was probably due to his sense of urgency. There was no time to waste: the end days marked by the second coming of Christ were imminent, and if they were to be hastened all Jews must convert. We must be prepared, Luther said, because in these last days the antichrist/devil is conspiring through many agents to have his way. Luther saw the antichrist everywhere: in the Vatican, that "institution of the devil"; among Moslems invading Europe; among Anabaptists, who rejected the eucharist; and among Jews, who rejected conversion. Of the Jews he preached, "if they could kill us all, they would fain do it, and often do so too."[21]

In the early days of his reform ministry, Luther's polemic was relatively tame. Not only was he hopeful for Jewish converts, but he was sufficiently aware of the failings of what he called "us wicked Christians" (including himself) to tolerate the existence of the Jews no matter how much he might mutter about "their" hard-heartedness. In other words, as long as Luther believed that Christianity still needed reforming, he did not deny the Jews' right to exist. But all this seeming tolerance was overthrown when he came to believe that Protestantism had triumphed and that he had won over sin, that he and his followers were no longer *reforming* but rather *reformed*.[22] Then he felt free to unleash an anti-Jewish polemic whose vituperativeness rivals that of John Chrysostom's homilies. "Gentle mercy will only tend to make them worse and worse, while sharp mercy will reform them but little," he wrote in the tract "On the Jews and Their Lies." "Therefore, in any case, away with them!"[23] Luther's attitude stands in striking contrast with the one expressed by his contemporary John Calvin when, in a sermon on Jeremiah 16:1–7, he said that the Jews only mirrored Christian rebellion against God: "when we read this passage, we appreciate that we should not condemn the Jews but ourselves."[24]

"Luther," says one of his biographers, "no longer let God be God."[25] The lesson seems clear: if Christians are to tolerate Jews as Jews, Christians must understand themselves as sinners. To do so means resisting the temptation to believe themselves to be exclusively, permanently, perfectly, and authoritatively saved.

8. THE ENLIGHTENMENT

The roots of antisemitism and all other "antis" lie in soil tilled by people who believe themselves to be possessors of absolute truth. Foremost among these people have been Christians, who have been able to enforce their beliefs throughout the west first through the agency of a mighty institutional church and later through the sheer number, wealth, and power of believers. Of course, many of those beliefs have been beneficial for Christians and non-Christians alike. But as we have seen, many were harmful to non-Christians, and especially to Jews. The church's language of intolerance has influenced any Christian who has paid even the least bit of attention to the teachings about the life and especially the death of Jesus. How hard it can be even for tolerant men and women to eradicate from their minds the anger that they were taught in their youth. If it is true that we never forget the prayers we learned as children, then it is equally true that we never forget the prejudices that accompanied those prayers.

However, if historic Christianity's involvement in antisemitism is so deep, how then do we explain the fact that the very worst persecution of the Jews occurred not under the medieval church but under a nation-state in the rational twentieth century? If the roots of antisemitism lie in the church's soil, in the centuries that we like to think of as modern, they are fertilized by a tradition that is decidedly anti-church: the great wave of rationalism and humanism called the enlightenment. No doubt, the enlightenment did away with many of the ancient prejudices and brought a new age of liberation and hope. One of the liberators was himself a Jew, Baruch Spinoza (1632–1677). After gaining a solid Jewish education, Spinoza was excommunicated by his synagogue in Amsterdam for claiming that not only was there no validity for the observance of the Torah, there was even less reason to hold religion as a foundation of human history. By the middle of the eighteenth century, French *philosophes* inspired by Spinoza were declaring that a new age of reason had come to eradicate superstition, prejudice, and blind faith. Practically this meant the end of the domination of the church in daily affairs. The ruling powers henceforth would be nations governed by the unfettered reasoning powers of free human beings.

That agenda would seem to be entirely beneficial. On its surface, it does away with the superstitions about Jews that were so widespread in the middle ages, and it encourages individual freedom. Unfortunately, this was far from the case. When it dealt with Jews, the rationalism of the enlightenment had a shadow side. No less than the church fathers and the crusaders, the *philosophes* set an absolute standard of what they perceived as being ideal behavior, and they expected all people, whether Christians, Jews, or pagans, to meet it. This universalism allowed no room for particularisms; all people were meant to drop their unique group identities and conform. In outline, this was not much of a change, for absolutism followed absolutism. In the middle ages the standard held up to humanity was Christian observance. In the enlightenment, it was adherence to the secular values of what the *philosophes* claimed was the age of greatest purity, enlightenment, and objectivity. That was the so-called golden age of Graeco-Roman civilization between the third century B.C.E. and the second century C.E. Any belief or behavior that strayed from that standard was condemned with the fervor of a Luther castigating the Jews for resisting conversion.

And so the age of anti-Judaism gave way to the age of antisemitism. Before, when all were expected to assimilate to the norms of the church, Jews were meant to become believing Christians. Now, when all were expected to behave "rationally," Jews were expected to live, look, and act not like semites but like Romans.

The humanists said that the Jews simply did not meet the standard because Jews were different. Instead of assimilating to "classical" norms, they were "orientals" who held themselves separate in dress, in language, and especially in religious practice. In these beliefs, the humanists harkened back to a classical line of thought which held that anybody who was different was automatically untrustworthy. In ancient Rome, where conformity was everything, Cicero had accused Jews of being clannish and disproportionately influential, had called Judaism a "superstitious barbarism," and had said it was a faith that "has nothing in common with the splendor of the empire, the gravity of our name, and the institutions of our ancestors." Difference meant disloyalty. Seneca went so far as to refer to the Jews as "this criminal people." In an earlier chapter we saw this Roman prejudice at work when the emperor Hadrian banned circumcision and threatened to give Jerusalem a pagan name.[26] Inspired by the classical call for conformity, the *philosophes* turned to Spinoza for contemporary justification of their attack on Jewish differences. Echoing an old antisemitic argument that the Jews were responsible for their own degradation, Spinoza claimed that Jews invited the world's contempt by continuing to separate themselves in appearance and customs.

Like the classicists, the neo-classicists of the eighteenth century accused Jews of disloyalty to absolute values of culture. While they claimed to be rational, the language of their criticism was purely polemic. Denis Diderot (1713–1784) accused the Jews of lacking "any rightness of thought, any exactness of reasoning or precision of style, in a word, any of that which ought to characterize a healthy philosophy. One finds among them . . . all the faults that mark an ignorant and superstitious people."[27] Going even further, Francois Marie Arouet de Voltaire (1694–1778) produced a contradictory attack on the Jews that saw them as both weak and strong at the same time. On the one hand, they were "a small, new, ignorant, crude people" whose ancestors had brought nothing of worth to civilization. Yet on the other hand, he asserted that they had a reservoir of immense power and danger, being born "with a raging fanaticism in their hearts, just as the Bretons and the Germans are born with blond hair." Jews, he went on, were "fated to be deadly to the human race."[28] Voltaire's schizophrenic polemic is a preview of the unfocused paranoia of the modern antisemite, who simultaneously sees the Jew as both worthless and threatening.

In this barrage of triumphant paganism, only a few voices could be heard protesting the absolutizing of pagan values and suggesting that Judaism had a place alongside other faiths in both ancient and modern civilization. The most prominent of the dissenters was Charles de Secondat Montesquieu (1689–1755). Writing from the standpoint of a Jew, he addressed the officials of the Spanish inquisition with this plea for toleration: "If you do not want to be Christians, at least be human: treat us as you would if you had neither a religion to guide or a revelation to enlighten you and had to act only on the basis of the weak intimations of justice with which nature endows us."[29] His was a lonely voice.

Thus the Christian absolutism of John Chrysostom and Martin Luther was replaced by a pagan absolutism. There were very profound and dangerous differences in the ways in which the old and new schools of thought regarded Judaism. Before, the Christians had attacked the Jews for something that "they" did: "they" poisoned wells and resisted conversion; above all, "they crucified the Lord." Now, however, the humanists focused their attention on *who the Jews were:* "they" were a fanatical, unreasoning people whose very character was one of opposition to the new, certain truth of enlightenment. (That this polemic was itself propounded fanatically and unreasoningly went unnoted; self-styled "humanists" are no more apt to be self-critical than are believers.) By being different from the run of Gentile society—e.g. by living in the communities of their ghettos, by observing the laws of their scripture and Talmud, by dressing in their own way and speaking their own language—all the Jews, in the eyes of the secular humanists, automatically qualified themselves not for respect but for contempt. In a phrase, Jews were disloyal to the new order of nationalistic, humanistic conformity.

In the words of the historian Arthur Hertzberg, these prejudices resolved themselves in a two-step conviction: first, the Jew was "irretrievably alien"; second, "all of society had to defend its purity against him." Writing with the holocaust a recent memory, Hertzberg adds that this racist conviction "was to recur many times, and in ever more dangerous forms, in the new age."[30]

Despite these deep prejudices, the enlightenment and the revolutions following in its wake led in the nineteenth century to the emancipation of many European Jews and others from the serfdom that had been imposed on them since the middle ages. The Jews of France were freed in the early 1790s, those of central Europe in 1848, and those of the Balkan countries in 1878. These emancipations were great events, but liberation came at a heavy price. In the name of their new, rational, humanistic, and egalitarian age, the liberators demanded that the Jews assimilate and abandon the special community customs and identities that had sustained Jewish peoplehood in the ghettos through all the years of official persecution. Even those who pointed out that the Jews' apparent debasement was due mostly to traditional anti-Jewish attitudes argued that in modern nations society must "raise the Jews to the level of educated and civilized people" and "develop among them the germ of social virtue."[31] The nationalists denied that Jewish culture in itself, apart from nationalism, had any redeeming features. Henceforth, identity would be defined by nationality. One could be French or Jewish, German or Jewish; but one could not be both. Since many Jews either wished to remain both or knew no other way to live than in the traditional Jewish manner, they were suspected of disloyalty.

The only place where enlightenment ideas about Judaism did not take hold was Russia. The descendants of the residents of the "Pale of Settlement," the provinces that Russia seized from Poland in the eighteenth century, remained enslaved or, at minimum, degraded. After the assassination of Czar Alexander II in 1881, a series of antisemitic riots called *pogroms* broke out. The government established a Jewish policy of thirds: one-third of the large Jewish population would be converted, one-third would be neglected until they died, and the remaining third would be allowed to emigrate. Many if not most of the emigrees fled across the Atlantic Ocean to the next way station in the diaspora, the United States. We now turn to the story of Jews in America.

NOTES

1. Franz Mussner, *Tractate on the Jews: The Significance of Judaism for Christian Faith,* Leonard Swidler, trans. (Philadelphia: Fortress, 1984), p. 47.

2. Rosemary Radford Ruether, *Disputed Questions: On Being a Christian* (Nashville: Abingdon, 1982), p. 71.

3. Edward Farley and Peter C. Hodgson, "Scripture and Tradition," in Peter C. Hodgson and Robert H. King, eds. *Christian Theology: An Introduction to Its Traditions and Tasks* (Philadelphia: Fortress, 1985²), p. 85.

4. Cf. Leon Poliakov, *The History of Anti-Semitism: From the Time of Christ to the Court Jews,* Richard Howard, trans. (New York: Schocken, 1974), p. 42.

5. *Ibid.,* p. 53.

6. *Ibid.,* p. 61.

7. *Ibid.,* p. 114.

8. *Ibid.,* p. 150.

9. Abraham J. Heschel, "The Mystical Element in Judaism," in Jacob Neusner, ed., *Understanding Rabbinic Judaism: From Talmudic to Modern Times* (New York: KTAV/ADL, 1974), pp. 294–295.

10. *Ibid.*

11. Quoted in Sholom Alchanan Singer, "The Book of the Pious," in Jacob Neusner, ed., *ibid.,* p. 303.

12. Max L. Margolis and Alexander Marx, *A History of the Jewish People* (New York: Temple/Atheneum, 1972), p. 564.

13. Chaim Potok, *The Chosen* (New York: Fawcett Crest, 1967), pp. 181–182.

14. John Calvin, "On Reform," in John Dillenberger, ed., *John Calvin: Selections from His Writings* (Missoula: Scholars Press, 1975), p. 93.

15. Pirke Aboth, IV:22, in R. Travers Herford, ed., *The Ethics of the Talmud* (New York: Schocken, 1962), p. 116.

16. S. Daniel Breslauer, "Salvation: Jewish View," in Leon Klenicki and Geoffrey Wigoder, eds., *A Dictionary of the Jewish Christian Dialogue* (New York/Mahwah: Paulist Press, A Stimulus Book, 1984), p. 182.

17. Martin Luther, "Preface to the New Testament," and "Preface to the Epistles of St. James and St. Jude," in John Dillenberger, ed., *Martin Luther: Selections from His Writings* (Garden City: Doubleday/Anchor, 1961), pp. 19, 36.

18. Cf. Eric W. Gritsch and Marc H. Tanenbaum, *Luther and the Jews* (New York: Lutheran Council in the USA, 1983), pp. 1–2, 7.

19. Cf. Heiko A. Oberman, *The Roots of Anti-Semitism in the Age of Renaissance and Reformation,* James I. Porter, trans. (Philadelphia: Fortress, 1984), p. 77.

20. Eric W. Gritsch and Marc H. Tanenbaum, *op. cit.,* p. 4.

21. *Ibid.*

22. Cf. Heiko A. Oberman, *op. cit.,* pp. 118–124.

23. Eric W. Gritsch and Marc H. Tanenbaum, *op. cit.,* p. 8.

24. Cf. Heiko A. Oberman, *op. cit.,* pp. 144–145, note 6, my trans.

25. Eric W. Gritsch and Marc H. Tanenbaum, *op. cit.,* p. 8.

26. Cf. Arthur Hertzberg, *The French Enlightenment and the Jews* (New York: Columbia University Press, 1968), p. 306.

27. *Ibid.,* pp. 311–312.

28. *Ibid.,* p. 237.

29. *Ibid.,* p. 300.

30. *Ibid.,* p. 367.

31. *Ibid.,* p. 334.

V. Jews in America and the Challenge of Religious Pluralism

The theme of Jewish-Christian relations in the United States is sum-marized in a "warning to Gentiles" that Milton Steinberg included in his book *Partisan Guide to the Jewish Problem.* Writing in 1945, just as the world was discovering the full truth about the Nazi war against the Jews, Steinberg insisted that Americans tended to be antisemitic not with the aggressive hatred of a Hitler but rather in a more muted way that stemmed from a lack of basic Gentile concern about Jews:

> I have in mind a widespread ambivalence concerning the Jews, a psy-chic tension between compassion and scruple on the one side, and antagonism on the other. Or to put it more concretely, I mean the mood of a non-Jew who is horrified by what Hitler has done and yet feels an impulse, of which to be sure he is ashamed, to applaud it; who regards Jew-baiting as disgraceful and yet wonders covertly whether it is not pretty much what "they" deserve; who protests against a *pogrom* but will neither employ Jews nor allow them into his country club.[1]

For a Christian who claims to be tolerant and who has read the previous chapters, Steinberg's warning must come as a slap in the face. Yet as we will see here, the depth, endurance, and effects of even this kind of ambivalent antisemitism must not be underestimated.

1. JEWS COME TO AMERICA

In the last years of the nineteenth and first years of the twentieth centuries, Jews fleeing from savage persecutions in Russia made up one of the greatest migrations in history. Some statistics hint at the importance of this movement. Russian immigration into the United States was less than one thousand people in 1870, just over thirty-five thousand in 1890, and more than one hundred and eighty-six thousand in 1910. Between 1870 and 1910 the Jewish population of New York City increased almost two thousand percent, from sixty thousand to more than one million. The proportion of Russians among children of foreign-born parents doubled every ten years, rising from less than two percent in 1900 to four percent in 1910 to almost six percent in 1920. By 1940 there were more children of Russian-born parents in the United States than there were children of English- and Welsh-born parents. In 1950 about eighty percent of the country's Jewish population was descended from people who had arrived after 1880.[2]

Today, approximately five and a half million Jews live in the United States, or slightly under three percent of the population. But the story of the Jews in America goes back far earlier than the mass Russian migration. Jews and American history have never been apart. The first Jews who settled in North America were a group of twenty-three "poor and healthy" refugees who fled a Dutch settlement in Brazil in 1654 after it was seized by the Portuguese. They were captured by Spanish pirates, from whom they were rescued by a French man-of-war, which carried them to the Dutch settlement of New Amsterdam. There the Jews hoped they would be welcomed by traditional Dutch tolerance. They were at first disappointed. The governor, Peter Stuyvesant, accused them of being "hateful enemies and blasphemers of Christ," but the Dutch West India Company, whose director included several Jews, eventually allowed them to stay with the proviso that they care for their own poor. At first they were permitted to engage only in wholesale trade, but within two years the Dutch permitted them to enter the retail trades. The next year these Jews formed the first public American synagogue and named it *Shearith Israel,* "the remnant of Israel."[3]

At the time of the American Revolution there were about one thousand Jews, most of them Sephardic, in the colonies. One of the largest and most successful Jewish communities was in Newport, Rhode Island, and its ups and downs provide a good picture of Jewish life in early America.

The Newport community came together in 1658. As elsewhere, many of the Jews were merchants or bankers continuing in the traditional professions imposed by the church in the middle ages. The Jewish population of the town rose with Newport's fortunes, a section of the town's cemetery was set aside for a Jewish burial ground, and in 1763 a beautiful colonial-style, octagonal house of worship was built to house Congregation Jeshuat Israel. However, as Newport's shipping fortunes fell after the American Revolution, the Jewish population moved to Providence, Boston, and other cities. By 1818 there were only three Jewish families in Newport, and the synagogue was in ruins. But hope survived. As he lay dying in Boston in 1823, a former Newport resident named Abraham Touro, a son of the synagogue's first cantor, declared it his wish to leave the state of Rhode Island ten thousand dollars to maintain the burial ground and restore the synagogue for use by Jews who, he hoped, would resettle in Newport.[4] The Touro Synagogue, as it came to be called, was made a national historical site, and today it is open to visitors on every day except Saturday, when the present-day Jewish community of Newport gathers to worship.

After 1800 there were several great waves of Jewish emigration from Europe to the United States that led not only to a vastly increased Jewish population but also to the development of four distinct branches of Judaism. While it would be an oversimplification to imply that Jewish "denominationalism" is a direct result of immigration differences, to use our limited space efficiently we will look at American Jewish history through its lens.

In 1826 approximately six thousand Jews were living in the United States. Judaism then could be described without adjectives: American Jews were Jews in a similar way that, in Europe before the reformation, all Christians were Christians. Most Jews in the United States of 1826 probably were Sephardic, that is, of Portugese and Spanish descent. By mid-century, however, the Jewish population had risen to fifty thousand after an enormous influx of Germans fleeing persecutions in central Europe, and with them came a strikingly new form of Judaism known as liberal or Reform Judaism.

First hinted at by the German philosopher Moses Mendelssohn (1729–1786), Reform Judaism was embraced by Jews who lived outside the ghettos, eager to share in the liberation of mind promised by the enlightenment, and hopeful of finding a meeting ground for the world and traditional Judaism. "The Jews were now modernized in their habits and tastes," generalizes historian Marc Lee Raphael, "and they wanted their Judaism to fit them as modern people; they wanted to assimilate Judaism to the modern Jew."[5] This point of view was not revolutionary, for, as we have seen, more than a thousand years earlier the rabbis who contributed to the Talmud were attempting to make the Torah relevant for contemporary Jews. Still, Reform Judaism met with considerable opposition as it evolved in Germany and then in the United States under such leaders as Rabbi Isaac Mayer Wise (1819–1900). As in religious conflicts between Christians, the polemic was intense; Wise spoke of "getting rid of all the medieval rubbish"—including the exclusive use of Hebrew, the repetition of prayers for the coming of the messiah, and the heightened role of the rabbi—and in 1850, in the middle of a Rosh HaShanah (new year's) service in his Albany, N.Y., congregation, Wise came to blows with the more orthodox president of his congregation.[6] He moved to Cincinnati where, in 1875, he helped found Hebrew-Union College as a seminary for training and ordaining Reform rabbis, and for deciding on theological matters. (A Jewish seminary serves the joint role shared in Christianity by a seminary and by a governing body, for example, a presbytery in the Presbyterian Church and the General Convention in the Episcopal Church.)

In 1885 American Reform rabbis gathered in Pittsburgh, Pa., to produce a statement of principles. Called by one of its authors the "Jewish Declaration of Independence" from the rabbinic tradition, the Pittsburgh Platform defined Judaism as a faith that is founded on monotheism and an ethical concern for justice and yet is ever open to changes that are guided by reason and scientific objectivity. The Pittsburgh Platform urged that this dynamic ethical monotheism not be limited either by an emphasis on Jewish peoplehood or by what was seen as a reliance on outworn religious practices—among which are the Halakah and lay submission to the authority of scholars and rabbis.[7] Some American Reform Jews, sensitive to the opinions of Christians living around them, developed forms of worship that were astonishingly assimilationist, going so far as to worship on Sunday, use English exclusively, refer to rabbis as "Jewish ministers," and engage choirs instead of cantors. That trend was long-lived. In the 1970s and 1980s many Reform congregations returned to more traditional practices, including the increased use of Hebrew. Yet Reform Judaism has continued on its liberalizing track in two significant areas. In 1982 the branch approved the ordination of women, and in 1983 it changed its definition of who is a Jew. A Jew has been traditionally understood to be the child of a Jewish mother, but with the increasing number of intermarriages the Reform branch has broadened the definition to include the child of a Jewish father. While some traditional Jews have since begun ordaining women, none have agreed with Reform Judaism's shift from exclusive matrilinealism.

In 1878 the Jewish population in the United States was three hundred thousand and consisted mainly of German and other central European Jews. By 1914 the figure had increased one thousand percent to three million, primarily because of immigration of Russian and Polish Jews. This mass migration was long, difficult, and painful—but it overflowed with hope. "The emigration fever was in its height in Polotzk, my native town," remembered young Mary Antin of the days before she and her family fled across the Atlantic in 1891:

"America" was in everybody's mouth. Businessmen talked of it over their accounts; the market women made up their quarrels that they might discuss it from stall to stall; people who had relatives in the famous land went around reading their letters for the enlightenment of less fortunate folks; the one letter-carrier informed the public how many letters arrived from America, and who were the recipients; children played at emigrating; old folks shook their sage heads over the evening fire, and prophesied no good for those who braved the terrors of the sea and the foreign goal beyond it;—all talked of it, but scarcely anybody knew one true fact about the magic land.[8]

These immigrants were a very different group from the free-thinking German Reform Jews. With the help of the Germans they settled in New York and other big cities, but most Russians had little taste for the liberal type of Judaism that they found in the Reform synagogues. If we are to believe young Mary Antin, America was infamous for how it transformed Judaism, for before she even left Russia she learned that "One sad fact threw a shadow over the splendor of the gold-paved, paradise-like fairyland. The travelers all agreed that Jews lived there in the most shocking impiety."[9] This became all too clear to a Hungarian rabbi named Moses Weinberger, who in 1887 wrote in despair about the reformers and their synagogues that he encountered in New York City:

Such is the nature of innovations these days: today it allows a man to do this, and tomorrow that. In the end he denies all, and makes of everything lofty, holy, and sublime one everlasting ruin. . . . The great and venerable congregation B[eth El] that now stirs up heaven and earth with its plans for a beautiful temple to be erected with due magnificence in the heart of the city, and which has already succeeded, with the assent of the great lights in Cincinnati and New York, in promulgating every new reform and in mercilessly uprooting all memories of that which has been precious to Israel since ancient times—this congregation just thirty years ago was holy and faithful.

Weinberger, like most opponents of change, blamed the loss of traditional faith on a new god: greed. "In America," he complained, "the basis and root of all is the dollar."[10]

Out of reactions like these grew an organized traditional Judaism that came to be called Orthodox Judaism. Orthodox Jews practice Halakah (for example, by keeping kosher kitchens and assiduously observing the sabbath), study the Talmud, respect the authority of rabbis and scholars, are committed to the idea of the peoplehood of Judaism, look forward to the coming of the messiah, are most apt to use Hebrew and read the mystical writings of the Cabbalah, and are least concerned about making an accommodation with the secular world. Their seminaries—Rabbi Isaac Elchanan Theological Seminary at Yeshiva University in New York, and Hebrew Theological College in Chicago—do not ordain women, and the sexes are separated in most Orthodox synagogues. Some groups in Orthodoxy oppose the establishment of the state of Israel because it was not brought about by the coming of the Messiah.

In 1924, after the great influx of Russian Jews around the turn of the century, Christian Americans of northern and western European stock pushed through an immigration reform bill that harshly limited immigration from eastern and southern Europe. However, after World War II the restrictions of that law were eased to allow refugees from the Nazis to enter. Among these were the Hasidic Jews of Poland, whose origins we looked at before. Now the best known and most separate of Orthodox Jews, the Hasidim live in their own self-supporting communities in and near large cities.

Of the original German Jewish immigrants, not all were Reform Jews. Those who were more traditional than the reformers and who also were more interested in "being American" than the orthodox found a large middle ground that came to be called Conservative Judaism. For Conservatives, Halakah remained important, as did Hebrew, the Talmud, and the authority of the rabbis and scholars. Conservative Judaism has been described as a "new synthesis of tradition and the modern spirit," and one Conservative rabbi has defined its fundamental philosophy somewhat mystically as "growth is the law of life, and Law is the life of Judaism."[11] Gerson D. Cohen, former Chancellor of Jewish Theological Seminary (Conservative Judaism's seminary), has defended an acculturationist attitude in language that challenges orthodoxy:

> We Jews have always been and will doubtless continue to be a minority group. But a minority that does not wish to ghettoize itself, one that refuses to become fossilized, will inevitably have to acculturate itself, i.e. to assimilate at least to some extent. If it wants to do business with the people among whom it lives, it will have to learn the spoken tongue, and it will have to re-orient its clothing and its style of life.[12]

As an example of this outlook, Jewish Theological Seminary now ordains women rabbis and women cantors.

The most distinctively American branch of Judaism is Reconstructionist Judaism. It began in the 1920s as a reform movement within Conservatism led by a rabbi and Jewish Theological Seminary professor named Mordecai M. Kaplan (1881–1983), whose goal was to change Judaism as a whole. Reconstructionism became a branch of its own when it opened its own seminary, in Philadelphia.

Kaplan observed that many American Jews were not attracted to any of the three established branches. He believed that none satisfied personal needs—Orthodoxy and Conservatism because they were too supernatural and hierarchical, and Reform because it was excessively dry and rational. Derogatorily comparing traditional Jewish metaphysics with alchemy and astrology, Kaplan dispensed with the ideas of a personal God, divine revelation, salvation after death, and the chosenness of the Jewish people. In response to the despair and disorderliness that he saw in modern life, he "reconstructed" Judaism to allow a God who is a positive force that brings creativity and unity to humanity. Kaplan wrote, "To believe in God is to reckon with life's creative forces, tendencies, and potentialities as forming an organic unity, and as giving meaning to life by virtue of that unity." God, he said, is "the power that endorses what we believe ought to be, and that guarantees that it shall be."[13]

Traditionalists were offended by Kaplan's denial of a personal God. An Orthodox rabbinical organization went so far as to claim the authority to excommunicate him from Judaism for "expressing atheism, heresy, and disbelief in the basic tenets of Judaism."[14] Yet, unlike the reformers, Kaplan did not sweep away ritual, which he saw as the glue that bonded Jew to Jew in community. Citing anthropological studies, he said that ritual is important because it brings people into community, and Jewish salvation lies in Jewish community. Halakah was important, too, but only when it was interpreted by the community for itself under the leadership of rabbis, and not by the rabbis for the community.

How popular are these branches? A survey in 1981 concluded that thirty-three percent of American Jews identify themselves as Conservative, nineteen percent describe themselves as Reform, and ten percent call themselves Orthodox (figures for Reconstructionism were not available). The remaining thirty-eight percent described themselves as "just Jewish," which means they have no preference and attend whatever synagogue is available (many communities cannot support more than one synagogue).[15]

Christians should be especially attentive to the last statistic. It suggests that Judaism is not a religion in the way that Christianity is a religion: it is not a system of beliefs in which various "denominations" emphasize one doctrine or another, but a peoplehood. While a church and a synagogue serve some similar purposes, they are different in crucial ways. A Christian denomination and a church bring together people of many backgrounds and a common theology; Judaism and a synagogue bring together people of one background and one or more theologies. For Jews there are no creeds and dogmas other than the simple statement of monotheism, the *Shema Israel* ("Hear, O Israel, the Lord thy God is one God"). For Christians there are creeds and dogmas, but there is nothing comparable to the Jewish idea of peoplehood. The synagogue, then, plays a larger role than the average parish church. "The synagogue is far more than a religious center," writes Charles S. Liebman. "It tends to be the center of all Jewish activity. . . . The synagogue is the institutional center of Jewish life."[16] Although the same could be said of some churches—for example, churches in urban black and immigrant communities—most members of mainline Christian denominations would probably describe their parishes solely as religious centers.

Reinforcing this observation, the 1981 survey came up with the following figures: one-half of American Jews belong to synagogues, yet only fourteen percent of American Jews worship weekly and only thirty-eight percent agree with the statement, "I know God really exists and I have no doubts about it." Since seventy-one percent of Christians surveyed were convinced that Jews are highly religious, these indications of Jewish religious ambivalence would come as a surprise to churchgoers. (Among Christians surveyed, forty-three percent attend church regularly and sixty-three percent ascribe to the statement of faith in God.)[17]

If this very brief overview suggests anything, it is that modern American Judaism (no less than early Judaism) is neither monolithic nor a mirror of Christianity. To say otherwise, as many Christians have done, is to try to make Judaism into something it is not, namely tamed, homogenized, and wholly predictable. Likewise, Judaism is anything but unified. Just as different Christian denominations sometimes look at each other as enemies, Orthodox Jews can be harshly critical of Reform and Conservative Jews, to the point of not recognizing their rabbis' authority and even reading them out of Judaism altogether. Any Christian who finds this strange is looking at Christianity through rose-tinted glasses.

2. ANTISEMITISM IN AMERICA

America was different. When two nineteenth century Jews wrote from New York to friends in China, they expressed astonishment at their new-found freedoms. "We in America, in New York and in other places, live in great security. Jews together with gentiles sit in judgment on civil and criminal cases."[18] We must share in their amazement, for compared with their lot in Europe most Jews who came to the United States were extremely well off. Not only has blatant antisemitism never been the policy of the national government, but American Gentiles have rarely descended to murderous Jew-baiting. As nasty as some people seemed at the time and as threatening as they appeared to Jews who knew all too well how a small posse could balloon into a large and dangerous *pogrom,* they did little to disturb the impression that in the United States, if nowhere else, Jews could live in freedom and safety.

Such would seem to remain the case. The Anti-Defamation League of B'nai B'rith reported in January 1987 that the number of antisemitic acts in the United States had decreased between 1981 and 1986, with a seven percent drop to 594 acts between 1985 and 1986, and with no reported Jew-baiting by far right-wing groups such as the Ku Klux Klan. In the fall of 1986, the A.D.L. tested antisemitic attitudes in a telephone survey of one thousand Christians, most of them in the "born-again" category of evangelicals and fundamentalists—the Christians usually thought to be most prejudiced against Jews. Eighty-six percent disagreed with the statement, recently voiced by a Southern Baptist leader, that "God does not hear the prayer of a Jew." Ninety percent disagreed with the statement, "Christians are justified in holding negative attitudes toward Jews, since the Jews killed Christ." In response to a query about their attitudes toward Jews, forty-nine percent said their attitudes were very or somewhat favorable, and only four percent admitted to having unfavorable attitudes. And while fifty-one percent said that "Jews are tight with money," most believed that was a positive trait.

And yet there is a certain insecurity. While the 1987 survey of antisemitic incidents indicated that the gross number was down, it also indicated that incidents on college campuses had more than tripled from six to nineteen since 1984. And while the 1986 telephone survey suggested that evangelicals and fundamentalists were open to Jews in some ways, it also produced some troubling results: fifty-nine percent agreed with the statement, "Jews can never be forgiven for what they did to Jesus unless they accept him as the true savior"; fifty percent said that Christians should work to convert Jews; twenty-seven percent felt that Jews are less loyal to the United States than to Israel; and twenty-seven percent believed that "because Jews are not bound by Christian ethics, they do things to get ahead that Christians do not generally do."[19]

What these contradictory statistics suggest is that American anti-semitism can be disguised by feelings of general good will, until it reveals itself in muted but clear patterns. Although the United States has seen no systematic persecution, the country does have a sustained tradition of prejudice that, because it usually is subtle, worries only people who suffer from it, and their friends. We can see the effects of this pattern of prejudice in many places. For example, note the small number of older Jews who are officers of banks and law firms, officials in the U.S. State Department, and graduates of prestigious universities such as Harvard and Yale. Until the 1950s, and in some cases later, all of those professions and institutions either banned Jews altogether or enforced rigid quotas. We also see prejudice in a history of restrictive social clubs, discriminatory real estate practices, and other observances of "the five o'clock shadow" —a phrase that means that while Jews may have equal rights with Gentiles in work life, they must go their own way when the office lights are turned off.[20] Thanks mostly to government action, all those areas have opened up since 1960. And yet the danger has not ended.

To understand the unease with which many Jews live in a country that, on the outside at least, seems to be the epitome of generosity and tolerance, we need look no further than the memories of older American Jews. In his moving memoir of uncovering his Jewish roots, *An Orphan in History,* the late Paul Cowan wrote this about his parents' insecurity:

> . . . I remembered my mother's childhood warnings that, for people like us, outward prosperity had nothing to do with real security. I remembered her admonition that I should learn a trade in case I had to flee to some foreign land, where my survival would be insured by a skill that didn't depend on language; I remembered my father urging Geoff and me to write letters to the F.B.I. telling them that our motives for going south [for civil rights work] were patriotic.[21]

These were not first generation immigrants living in poverty in the 1890s. The time was the 1950s and 1960's, and Cowan's father was president of C.B.S. Television.

The insecurity of Paul Cowan's parents indicates that the kind of antisemitism described by Milton Steinberg at the outset of this chapter is still alive and well in the United States. Here we will attempt to see the outlines of this intolerance by looking at ways in which it has surfaced in American history.

American antisemitism falls into two familiar patterns of absolutism. One is the traditional theological anti-Judaism that declares that the truth resides solely in Christianity, and that Jews are guilty of opposing and even killing that truth. While this prejudice has sometimes been vicious, it has usually been less blatant than it was in medieval Europe. The other pattern is a steady attack on Jewish patriotism and trustworthiness. This pattern corresponds to the enlightenment's passion for assimilation to nationalistic, majority values. Here it defends something called "Americanism"—those values and behavior of native, white, Gentile Protestants who regard Jews, Roman Catholics, and other immigrants as "aliens" who seem to challenge a nativist idea of normative citizenship and behavior. Because both patterns involve religious attitudes and postures, the Christian argument against Judaism remains important even in the United States, the first nation to forbid "any law respecting an establishment of religion, or prohibiting the free exercise thereof" (the First Amendment to the Constitution). We shall begin with gross examples of American antisemitism, and then conclude with the subtle kind, about which too many Gentiles are insensitive.

The American colonies all limited the legal rights of Jews, using a variety of approaches. Some colonies followed the old tradition of squashing religious freedom. For example, a Maryland law required that anybody who denied Jesus' divine Sonship or the Trinity "should for the first offense be fined and have his tongue bored"; the punishment for the third offense was death.[22] In most cases, however, the focus was on limiting the voting rights of Jews. Geography played no favorites. Rhode Island, founded by the great defender of religious freedom Roger Williams, granted Jews freemanship in 1665; but in 1728 Williams' successors withdrew political rights, which were not restored until 1842. Colonial Virginia barred Jews from appearing in court as witnesses, New York banned Jews from voting for the state assembly, and South Carolina, although it elected a Jew to the first provincial congress, prohibited Jews from voting altogether.

After the American Revolution, the general attitude of the new nation toward Jews was mixed. To judge by the U.S. Constitution, they were the equals of all men and women; to judge by many state laws, they were regarded as unqualified for citizenship; and to judge by the energetic efforts of missionary societies, they were fully capable of becoming members of society if only they converted to Christianity. The anti-Jewish legislation of the colonies survived the Revolution, and in some cases long survived it. For a while the state constitutions of Massachusetts, Maryland, and North Carolina prohibited Jews from holding public office. The latter two states also banned them from the legal profession. North Carolina did not grant complete political rights until 1868, while, up in "tolerant" New England, New Hampshire did not allow them these rights until 1877. To put this tardy democracy in context, in Great Britain where Jews had not even been permitted to live until 1661, and where there was (and remains) an established national church, non-Christians were permitted to be members of parliament in 1866, eleven years before Jews were finally given political rights throughout the United States.

Political rights were one thing. The right to remain unchallenged as Jews was something else. In 1820 the Rev. Joseph Samuel C. F. Frey, a convert from Judaism who had recently arrived from Britain, applied to the state of New York for a charter for an organization called the American Society for Colonizing and Evangelizing the Jews, which would bring other converts from Europe to settle in Jewish-Christian colonies. The state rejected the name on the grounds that it was sectarian. Frey found a new and more bland substitute: the American Society for Meliorating the Condition of the Jews. After the colonization plans collapsed due to an insufficient number of converts, the society became an agency not for improving the social lot of Jews but for converting the increasing population of American Jews to Christianity. This was not readily apparent to Jews fooled by the names both of the society and of its magazine, *Israel's Advocate,* which was little more than a running attack on Jewish principles.

Frey and his society believed that their efforts were a major advance over the traditional Christian anti-Jewish posture. Love, not contempt, was the society's motivation. If sufficient degrees of love were shown for their misled Jewish brothers and sisters, who knew how many converts would flock to the church? In the society's annual report of 1843, the officers wrote:

> Let us honestly confess it—the prejudice and bigotry have been ours scarcely less than theirs, and why should we wonder at the result? But approach a Jew (as we have recently been led to do) in the spirit of kindness and Christian love, visit him in his duress, speak comfortably

to him, let him see that we desire to relieve his wants, and we find that he has the heart of a man, and that it will respond to our own. . . . What a revolution is here begun in the Jewish heart![23]

That revolution, of course, was apostasy.

Other than the accurate and long overdue criticism of historic Christianity's attitude about Judaism, there was nothing new in this attitude. Jews remain hard, distressed, legalistic people stuck in antiquity and needful of transformation brought only by Christian love. This archetype seems to be universal among Gentiles wishing to manage the lives of Jews. We see it in just about every statement by a Christian that begins, "The Jew is . . ." Most Christians would be deeply offended by a sentence that begins, "The Christian is . . ."—yet patronizing generalizations about Jews are part of many Christians' daily talk. The historian Jonathan D. Sarna has aptly described the archetype as the "mythical Jew," which inevitably must conflict with the reality of the "Jew next door." Referring specifically to the nineteenth century, but aiming his comments at all history, Sarna writes:

Highly intelligent American Christians faced the same problem: how to reconcile the "mythical Jew," found in the Bible, recalled in church, and discussed in stereotypic fashion, with the "Jew next door" who seemed altogether different. Mythical Jews could, depending on the circumstances, personify either evil or virtue. Real Jews fell somewhere in between. Mythical Jews were uniformly alike. Real Jews displayed individuality, much as most people do.[24]

Very often, the two images of the Jew, one based on fantasy and the other on reality, could not be reconciled, and the resulting tension led back to the same old contempt that missionizing Christians thought they were ending.

As throughout Christian history, the attempt to convert large numbers of Jews was a failure. Quickly seeing through the guise of loving friendship made by the American Society for Meliorating the Condition of the Jews, many Jews sprang to a brisk counterattack, both in a book titled *Israel Vindicated* and in the first Jewish magazine in America, *The Jew* (subtitled *Being a Defense of Judaism against all Adversaries, and particularly against the insidious attacks of Israel's Advocate*). The society, argued the anonymous author of *Israel Vindicated,* was nothing more than a new expression of traditional intolerance. It "erected a barrier, which, if not broken down, must forever expose the Jews of this country, to obloquy and contempt, for their adherence to that form of worship which, only, they considered divine."

3. PROTECTIVE NATIVES

Elsewhere in Christian America, Judaism was widely regarded as a synonym for untrustworthiness. A Christian's political persuasion was no predictor of his or her attitude about Jews: the famous abolitionist William Lloyd Garrison called one rabbi a "lineal descendant of the monsters who nailed Jesus to the cross between two thieves,"[25] and at their general convention in 1844, the bishops of the Episcopal Church echoed Luther in attacking Roman Catholic practices as being like ancient Jewish sacrifices, "in deadly error."[26]

If any single factor tamed American antisemitism before 1890, it was perhaps because Jews were vastly outnumbered by, and therefore much less noticeable than, blacks and Roman Catholics. American nativists in the Know-Nothing Party, reading "Protestant" for "Christian," persecuted Catholic immigrants with a crusader's vengeance. For example, a mob incited by the Rev. Lyman Beecher destroyed a convent in Massachusetts in 1834; ten years later two Philadelphia Catholic churches were burned and thirteen people were killed in an anti-Catholic riot. In 1887 a Methodist and thirty-second degree Mason named Henry F. Bowers founded the American Protective Association because, he said, "I have been raised up by the Almighty God to do a great work for the country and for human freedom."[27] The "great work" that Bowers referred to in this declaration, so similar in its mixture of religion and patriotism to the statements of German churchmen who followed Hitler in the 1930s, was to fight the power of the Roman Catholic Church, which Bowers found wherever things seemed to be going wrong for him. By the depression year of 1893, the membership of the A.P.A. was at least one hundred thousand.

Even though Catholicism became the largest community of Christians, thanks to people much less crazy-sounding than Bowers, Catholics were rarely permitted the luxury of believing that they could assert the political and social power that usually comes with large numbers. When an Episcopal priest participated in a synagogue service in Maryland in 1851, the bishops were merely scandalized. But if his agenda had included a Roman Catholic mass he might have been excommunicated.[28]

Violent outbreaks of antisemitism in the United States have been relatively few, and most took place during the great wave of Russian immigration after about 1890. Some historians believe that these riots were stimulated not by religious beliefs but by economic changes that left previously secure groups of Americans distressed by shifts in social status. Suddenly marginalized people such as farmers, patrician New Englanders, and urban industrial workers lashed out at the vulnerable newcomers. Since people who attacked newcomers considered themselves natives, this conflict was called nativism.[29]

While the nativist theory of prejudice has its merits, it has been justifiably criticized because it discounts the importance of religious beliefs long held by Christians; in doing so, it claims that American antisemitism was not in continuity with the European experience.[30] From the point of view of nativism, antisemitism is not much different from anti-Catholicism. Both are part of a generalized attack by native Protestant residents on anybody who is different, and especially on anybody whose fortunes are improving while the nativists' fortunes are declining.[31]

No doubt there is some truth in this, and events bear it out. For example, patrician Protestant Anglo-Saxons led a drive for restrictions on immigrants from southern and eastern Europe on the grounds, inspired by recently developed theories about eugenics, that Jews were racially inferior by the norms of British and Scandinavian immigrants. Jews, they said, were physically weak—as one nativist put it, "On the physical side the Hebrews are the polar opposite of our pioneer breed"—and intellectually retarded. The early I.Q. tests, established mainly to prove Gentile superiority, indicated that a large majority of Jewish immigrants were feeble-minded. Jews were also believed to be carriers and breeders of diseases in the ghettos.

In reaching these "scientific" conclusions about racial inferiority, the nativists not only refused to consider environmental factors such as historic malnutrition, poverty, and language problems, but also relied on inaccurate information. Recent studies of health, mortality, and other relevant data for the period 1880–1914 indicate that many of those perceptions were false. Jenna Weissman Joselit has found that Jewish death rates in Boston and New York were lower than those of both the native population and northern European immigrants, and that Jews were no more likely to be institutionalized for mental illness than Italians, Germans, and the Irish. Simon Kuznets has discovered that, compared both with other immigrants and with the Jews who stayed behind, male Jews from Russia were well educated, with literacy rates of over eighty percent compared with about seventy-four percent for non-Jewish male immigrants; female Jewish immigrants were less well educated than female non-Jewish immigrants. These rates are for literacy in the native language.

If literacy is one indication of aptitude, commitment is another: Kuznets found that while thirty-two percent of non-Jewish immigrants departed the United States in the period 1908–1914, usually after a few years' residence, only seven percent of Jewish immigrants did so.[32] Whether or not that was because they had no other place to go, the ninety-three percent Jewish retention rate speaks volumes about the compatibility of the United States and Jewish hopes.

The restriction lobby was powerful, and the immigration act of 1924 established an annual immigration quota equal to two percent of a nationality's population in the 1890 census. Since most Jews had come after 1890, this law had a severe impact. After World War II, President Harry Truman directed that special provisions be made to allow the immigration of large numbers of displaced persons.

As another example of nativism, antisemitism was significant in the late nineteenth and early twentieth century Populist movement, in which farmers fought against dropping prices, high tariffs, and other factors that were destroying their livelihoods. Antisemitic political figures such as Tom Watson encouraged many poverty-striken farmers to blame Jews for their woes with claims that Jews were behind a great international conspiracy of financiers to transform the world by industrialization.

Related to nativism was the antisemitism of fairly recent immigrants who struggled to find secure homes and jobs in the growing cities and industries, only to see that security challenged by the newcomers. Jew-baiting by the Irish, Germans, and others was so bad that in many cities Jews formed their own protective associations. "No Jew here can go on the street without exposing himself to the danger of being piteously beaten," Brooklyn Jews complained in 1899.[33] Three years later, on Manhattan's lower east side, some two hundred people were injured when Irish workers, and later Irish policemen, attacked Jews marching in a funeral procession for a deceased rabbi.

4. "CHRISTIAN AMERICA"

Social nativism, however, was just part of the picture. Religious-based antisemitism existed much earlier than the massive Russian-Jewish migration. This does not mean that American antisemitism is simply an extension of European prejudice. America's unique contribution to the problem may well be that, here, intolerance frequently flows from people like William Lloyd Garrison who perceive themselves and are generally seen as being the epitome of tolerance. A factor in this seeming paradox may well be the typical American understanding of the meaning of the word "tolerance," which in a society of such extraordinary diversity often means nothing more than common politeness of the "I'm O.K., you're O.K." variety. People who would never be rude to a Jew, or to anybody else, boast of their conquest of bigotry even as they make no effort to reach the true tolerance that comes with an understanding of the other person's deepest convictions. In a phrase, the attack on *Judaism* has often been aided by people who would never attack *a Jew.* This paradoxical marriage of civility toward Jews as individuals with intolerance for their beliefs has been repeated time and again, most recently by Gentile anti-Zionists who refuse to understand how important Israel is to most Jews, and by Christians who do not know how insulting it is to claim, "Some of my best friends are Jews."

An excellent example of this paradox is Thomas Jefferson. His passion for religious freedom lives on in the First Amendment and the disestablishment clause in the U.S. Constitution. Yet he also asserted that the Jewish idea of God was "degrading and injurious," and he condemned Jewish ethics as "imperfect," "often irreconcilable with the sound dictates of reason and morality," and "repulsive and antisocial." Speaking of Jews with the injudicious, sweeping "they" that characterizes unconscious antisemitism, Jefferson concluded that "they needed reformation, therefore, in an eminent degree."[34]

In a broader picture, we see this paradox repeated in Gentile attitudes about the legal foundations of the United States. For example, in his commentary on the U.S. Constitution, published in 1833, Supreme Court Justice Joseph Story (1779–1845) had nothing but good to say about the ban on religious tests for public office (Article VI, Section 3). Of the founding fathers' decision to include this prohibition in the Constitution, this self-styled "sturdy defender of religious freedom of opinion" made an eloquent statement that deserves to be displayed in every school and church:

> They knew, that bigotry was unceasingly vigilant in its stratagems, to secure to itself an exclusive ascendancy over the human mind; and that intolerance was ever ready to arm itself with all the terrors of the civil power to exterminate those, who doubted its dogmas, or resisted its infallibility.

Nevertheless, four years earlier this same Joseph Story declared: "Christianity is a part of the Common Law. . . . There never has been a period in which the Common Law did not recognize Christianity." In 1844, speaking for the Supreme Court in the landmark case of *Vidal v. Girard's Executors,* Story said that a school's benefactor could prohibit clergy from teaching classes in morals so long as there was no ban on teaching the New Testament, the source of "the purest principles of morality." However, Story continued, it would have been an entirely different matter had the donor specified that Christianity be repudiated or not be taught at all, or that a school be established "for the propagation of Judaism, or Deism, or any other form of infidelity."[35]

If Story and Jefferson could be excused, it would be because they lived in a day before the United States was sufficiently pluralistic to channel into daily practice the forward-looking theories of democratic diversity that lay behind the Constitution. "While the law allows the American people to do everything," Alexis de Tocqueville observed then, "there are things which religion prevents them from imagining and forbids them to dare."[36] Today the context is very different. Anybody who continues to believe with Joseph Story that this is "a Christian country," where "Christian" prayers and symbols must be imposed on all, flies in the face of the obvious religious pluralism that has been one of God's gifts to the United States. The church historian Robert T. Handy has aptly described the country as being, religiously, "a Catholic-Jewish-Orthodox-Protestant-Mormon-Pentecostalist-New Thought-Humanist nation," adding that most of these options can themselves be further subdivided.[37] Whichever group takes it upon itself to select religious symbols to be imposed on all—for example, the words to be used in required school prayers—must realize that somebody's rights, beliefs, and principles will be deeply offended no matter which symbols are chosen. It is not sufficient to think in terms of majority rule, for example, by citing "the Judeo-Christian tradition," a phrase suggesting that, once again, Christians are appropriating Judaism for Christianity's own purposes. As the sorry history of attempts to destroy Judaism make very clear, in religion "majority" does not automatically equal "truth."

A few people saw the dangers in the claims for "a Christian America." One was the memorable Zebulon Vance (1830–94), the Confederate governor of North Carolina and later a U.S. senator. Vance spent much of his free time between 1874 and 1890 traveling to southern towns and lecturing against antisemitism in both its theological and enlightenment forms. The deicide argument, he said insightfully, "unconsciously lays a foundation of prejudice, which is largely added to by the jealousy of Gentile rivals in business. Nothing is so satisfactory to a man as to be able to excuse an unworthy motive by referring it to a love of God and his religion." As for the criticism of Jewish "otherness" he attacked "the unreasonable propensity to consider the Jew under all circumstances as a foreigner, in which case we veneer our motive with a love of country."[38]

5. THE LEO FRANK AFFAIR

The antisemitism that Zebulon Vance identified and battled surfaced violently in the Leo Frank affair. In 1913 a thirteen year old Atlanta, Georgia girl named Mary Phagan was found dead in a pencil factory. The police soon after arrested the factory's superintendent and part-owner, Leo Frank, on trumped-up and circumstantial evidence. Frank's arrest was popular. The fact that he was an industrialist reputed to underpay his employees seemed indirectly to confirm the charges; that he was also a Jew made the charges even more believable. A writer surveying public opinion about the case reported, "One man, after asserting that there is no prejudice against Frank because he is a Jew, grows eloquent and says Mary Phagan is our folks."[39] Frank's lawyers were not able to convince the jury that he was the victim of a crude frame-up, and he was found guilty of the murder. (In 1986, conclusive evidence that Frank was framed finally appeared.) The death sentence was later commuted on appeals aided by the American Jewish Committee, an organization devoted to protecting American Jews that was founded in 1906. But spurred on by the antisemitic ravings of the Populist leader Tom Watson, Georgians did not forget the case. A fellow prison inmate attacked and almost killed Frank with a butcher's knife. Outside the prison walls, a mob that called itself the Knights of Mary Phagan gathered at the girl's grave and swore vengeance, and on August 16, 1915 they kidnaped Frank from prison and lynched him.

Around the time of the Frank trial and lynching, two new and very different organizations were formed that have since greatly affected Christian-Jewish relations in the United States. One reflected a sense of triumph, the other a sense of fear.

A few weeks after the lynching, some three dozen triumphant members of the Knights of Mary Phagan reformed the old Ku Klux Klan, which the historian Leonard Dinnerstein has described as "dedicated to the everlasting exaltation of southern heroism, chivalry, and Anglo-Saxon splendor; an organization that would work for the revival of rural, Protestant culture; an organization which shunned the alien, put the Negro in his place, and elevated the Anglo-Saxon American to his rightfully superior niche in American society."[40] With its intimidating white costume, crossburnings, and lynch ropes, the K.K.K. created a sensation, and the filmmaker D. W. Griffith immediately celebrated it in his film *The Birth of a Nation.* While the K.K.K. concentrated its agenda on terrifying southern blacks, it had a strong antisemitic component. It eventually spread to the north and is now especially strong in western Connecticut.

The other new organization took southern antisemitism, as revealed in the Frank case, seriously enough to fear for all American Jewry. A month after Leo Frank was found guilty in 1913, the Jewish fraternal order B'nai B'rith (Children of the Covenant) formed the Anti-Defamation League to combat the kind of Jew-baiting that so heavily flavored the trial. Since then, the A.D.L. has been an assiduous watchdog for antisemitism from all corners, whether it is an aspect of the anti-communism of the political right or the anti-Zionism of the political left. Besides drawing public attention to antisemitic activity, the A.D.L.'s annual reports and other publications have also provided a reliable measure of American hate activity against blacks and other minorities.[41]

A recurring Christian response to the A.D.L. and other Jewish defense groups has been to blame them for the troubles that Jews suffer. This deserves some comment. Such criticisms usually begin with phrases like "If the Jews had been content . . ." and "If the Jews had left well enough alone. . . ." For example, twelve years after the Frank trial an Atlanta journalist suggested that without the pressure of the American Jewish Committee, all would be well for Jews: "If the Jews had been content to regard Frank as a man suspected of murder, entitled to a fair trial and nothing more, instead of a Jew on the threshold of martyrdom, hounded by Christians thirsting for his blood, there would have been little or no antisemitic feeling in Atlanta."[42]

While there is no question that people can bring troubles on themselves, it is illogical to say that prejudice is self-inflicted by a desire for justice on the part of those who are the victims of prejudice. This claim echoes the old charge that Jews make themselves responsible for antisemitism by being different from Christians, that is, by being Jews. If antisemitism is defined as hatred of all Jewish people solely because of who they are and how they behave as Jews, then antisemitism must also be the term used to describe attacks on attempts by Jews to defend their right to live as Jews.

After the Frank trial, antisemitism became an integral part of a certain kind of right-wing polemic that portrayed Americans as victims under a vast international Jewish conspiracy. In the 1920s Henry Ford was eagerly distributing copies of *The Protocols of the Elders of Zion,* a forged document that first appeared in czarist Russia to "prove" that the world was being destroyed by Jewish financiers. In the 1930s Jew-baiters searching for a cause of the Great Depression found equally believable tales of a Jewish-communist conspiracy to take over the world, inspired by the fact that some prominent socialists and communists were Jewish. One of the most prominent antisemites was a Catholic priest named Charles E. Coughlin, who for several years broadcast over the radio hate-filled sermons about what he perceived as the Jewish-communist menace.

As usual, beneath this highly dramatic kind of antisemitism lay a more subtle, latent variety that revealed itself less in attacks on Jews than in apathy about Jewish problems. It surfaced in American Christians' lack of action to help Jews escape from Hitler's Germany in the 1930s. While American Jewish groups raised millions of dollars to help Jews emigrate from Germany and lobbied hard to get the U.S. government to make exceptions to the strict quotas established by the 1924 immigration act, most Protestants did little beyond making very occasional statements of concern. Christian as well as Jewish refugees received little attention. Between 1939 and 1941, the Episcopal Church's Presiding Bishop's Fund for World Relief was able to raise only $20,000 to give to Christian refugee organizations; an appeal to five thousand parishes by the General Council of the Congregational Christian Churches for funds to help Christian refugees raised only $427 from twenty-eight churches.

Many people honestly believed that Depression America could not absorb a large number of impoverished refugees, and yet while a bill allowing Jewish child refugees to enter languished in Congress, there was little opposition to a special dispensation to allow English children to come over to escape the Blitz. Most people who did actively help did so either out of a general commitment to social action or out of a personal connection with Jews. Ironically, one concerned group that fit into both categories was that of evangelicals working to convert Jews. Otherwise, to quote an authority, "The great body of American Protestants remained indifferent and for the most part failed to become fully aroused by the plight of the Nazi victims or to appreciate the moral dimensions involved."[43]

The knowledge of the holocaust came as a shock and tempered antisemitic activity after World War II, at least partly because many Christian religious leaders made a conscious effort to steer their people in the direction of tolerance and understanding. Still, the sense of Jewish "otherness" obstructed true dialogue. The Protestant attitude of the time was well summarized in an editorial comment made in 1952 by the mainline, liberal religious magazine *The Christian Century*. The editors objected to the choice of New York City as the site of the new headquarters of the National Council of Churches, a Protestant ecumenical body, on the grounds that the city was an "alien and demoralizing environment" where the Protestant population was outnumbered ten to one by Jews and Roman Catholics. The editors felt that as a minority, the N.C.C. would become unduly defensive.[44]

After a period of relative peace that saw a beginning of Christian-Jewish dialogue, in the early 1960s some six hundred American synagogues were desecrated with swastikas, while armed gangs swaggered around the countryside in the name of states' rights, white people's rights, Christian identity, and the American Nazi party. Later in the decade, antisemitic statements began to be made publicly by black leaders. This was extremely disturbing to many Jews who had long sympathized with black suffering and supported civil rights and black self-help organizations. Many people believed that the outburst was no more than a symptom of old economic inequities in which the Jews were caught in the middle: the release of the long-building frustration of urban blacks against Jewish landlords and shopkeepers who were seen as exploiting them, even though the Jews themselves were exploited by white Gentiles.

Yet as is so often the case with antisemitism, the truth probably has more to do with religion than with economics. By the late 1960s some blacks simply felt free to repeat in public what many devout Christian blacks were taught to say in the privacy of churches and homes. As the novelist Richard Wright put it in *Black Boy,* "All of us black people who lived in the neighborhood hated Jews, not because they exploited us but because we had been taught at home and in Sunday school that Jews were 'Christ killers.' "[45] As had happened since the middle ages, the Shylockian polemic about "money-grubbing," "usurous" and "unscrupulous" Jews followed right after the Christian diatribes.

Synagogue desecrations, Jew-baiting, insensitive comments, misreadings of Jewish concerns, and other forms of blatant and subtle forms of antisemitism continue to recur in our decade, but perhaps more noticeable have been four new developments that have unsettled relations between Christians and Jews. First, a California-based organization with the academic-sounding name of the Institute for Historical Review spent its days and nights telling the world that the holocaust never took place. Second, some black leaders engaged in nasty Jew-baiting that went far beyond traditional antisemitism; for example, a Black Moslem leader named Louis Farakan called Judaism a "gutter religion" and praised Hitler as a "great man." Third, despite its long-standing defense of Jews and Jewish causes (at least partly because many Jews were active in liberal, socialist, and reform organizations), the political left began, in the 1970s to mouth antisemitisms in the guise of a virulent anti-Zionism. Fourth, as the left seemed to be abandoning the Jews, some leaders of that traditional stronghold of antisemitism, the religious right, were exhibiting a surprising support for Israel and Judaism in general and even going so far as to reject the deicide tradition. (However, this last step was not complete, for Jerry Falwell substituted a claim that "all persons in every age," including Jews, "must share in the blame for Christ's death."[46]

In our frustration at these turnabouts we should recall how, in the early 1960s, the prejudices of antisemites were confirmed when many Jews became involved with the civil rights movement, which, among other benefits, turned out to be one of the first and best agencies of the Jewish-Christian dialogue that we will presently describe in more detail. Martin Luther King, Jr. welcomed Jewish help and consistently held up Jews as examples of a people who had survived and even thrived despite terrible repression. In his 1967 book *Where Do We Go from Here: Chaos or Community?* King criticized the tendency among blacks to believe that American Jews have succeeded only because of money. King argued that this encourages both antisemitism and materialism, and went on to identify a key component of historic Judaism that kept the Jewish people alive:

> Jews progressed because they possessed a tradition of education combined with social and political action. The Jewish family enthroned education and sacrificed to get it. The result was far more than abstract learning. Uniting social action with educational competence, Jews became enormously effective in political life. Those Jews who became lawyers, businessmen, writers, entertainers, union leaders, and medical men did not vanish into the pursuits of their trade exclusively. They lived an active life in political circles, learning the techniques and arts of politics. Nor was it only the rich who were involved in social and political areas. They lived in homes in which politics was a household word. They were deeply involved in radical parties, liberal parties, and conservative parties—they formed many of them. Very few Jews sank into despair and escapism even when discrimination assailed the spirit and

corroded initiative. Their life raft in the sea of discouragement was social action.[47]

The lesson is for us all.

NOTES

1. Milton Steinberg, *A Partisan Guide to the Jewish Problem* (LanHam: University Press of America, 1986²), p. 37.
2. Statistics in *Historical Statistics of the United States* (Washington: U.S. Bureau of the Census, 1960), pp. 56, 65.
3. Max L. Margolis and Alexander Marx, *A History of the Jewish People* (New York: Temple/Atheneum, 1972), pp. 603–605.
4. The bequest is printed in Joseph L. Blau and Salo W. Baron, eds., *The Jews in the United States, 1790–1840: A Documentary History* (New York and Philadelphia: Columbia University Press-Jewish Publication Society, 1963), vol. iii, pp. 832–833.
5. Marc Lee Raphael, *Profiles in American Judaism: The Reform, Conservative, Orthodox and Reconstructionist Traditions in Historical Perspectives* (San Francisco: Harper & Row, 1984), p. 6.
6. *Ibid.,* p. 13.
7. *Ibid.,* pp. 13, 16.
8. Mary Antin, ed., *From Plotzk to Boston* (New York: Markus Wiener, 1986), pp. 11–12.
9. *Ibid.,* p. 12.
10. Jonathan D. Sarna, ed., *People Walk on Their Heads: Moses Weinberger's Jews and Judaism* (New York: Holmes & Meier, 1981), pp. 64–65.
11. Cf. Marc Lee Raphael, *op. cit.* pp. 92, 104.
12. Gerson D. Cohen, "The Blessings of Assimilation in Jewish History," in Jacob Neusner, ed., *Understanding Jewish Tradition: Classical Issues and Modern Perspectives* (New York: KTAV-ADL, 1975), p. 255.
13. Cf. Marc Lee Raphael, *op. cit.,* p. 182.
14. *Ibid.,* p. 184.
15. Gregory Martire and Ruth Clark, *Anti-Semitism in the United States: A Study of Prejudice in the 1980's* (New York: Praeger, 1982) p. 99.
16. Charles S. Liebman, "The Religion of American Jews," in Jacob Neusner, ed., *Understanding American Judaism: Toward the Description of a Modern Religion* (New York: KTAV/ADL, 1975), vol. I, p. 49.
17. Gregory Martire and Ruth Clark, *op. cit.,* p. 99.
18. Cf. Yuri Suhl, *An Album of the Jews in America* (New York: Watts, 1972), p. 23.
19. Survey of incidents in "Report on Anti-Semitism," in the Stamford, Connecticut *Advocate,* Jan. 23, 1987; opinion survey in "Attitude Toward Jews," in *The Christian Century,* Jan. 21, 1987, p. 49.

20. I will never forget the shock I felt when I heard a speaker at a college fraternity orientation announce, "We have twelve fraternities: six Jewish and six Christian."

21. Paul Cowan, *An Orphan in History: Retrieving a Jewish Legacy* (Garden City: Doubleday, 1982), pp. 141–142.

22. Cf. Leonard Dinnerstein and Mary Dale Palsson, eds., *Jews in the South* (Baton Rouge: Louisiana State University Press, 1973), p. 5.

23. Cf. Jonathan D. Sarna, "Jewish-Christian Hostility in the United States," in Robert N. Bellah and Frederick E. Greenspahn, eds., *Uncivil Religion: Interreligious Hostility in the United States* (New York: Crossroad, 1987), p. 8.

24. Jonathan D. Sarna, "The 'Mythical Jew' and the 'Jew Next Door,' " in David A. Gerber, ed., *Anti-Semitism in American History* (Urbana: University of Illinois Press, 1986), p. 58.

25. Cf. Joseph L. Blau and Salo W. Baron, eds., *op. cit.,* vol. III, p. 759.

26. Cf. Jonathan D. Sarna, "Jewish-Christian Hostility in the United States," *op. cit.,* p. 15.

27. E. Clowes Chorley, *Men and Movements in the American Episcopal Church* (Hamden: Archon, 1966), p. 221.

28. Cf. John Higham, *Send These to Me: Jews and Other Immigrants in Urban America* (New York: Atheneum, 1975), p. 74.

29. E. Clowes Chorley, *op. cit.,* p. 274.

30. This theory has been best expressed by historians in the progressive-liberal tradition; cf. especially Richard Hofstadter, *The Age of Reform* (New York: Knopf, 1955); and John Higham, *Strangers in the Land: Patterns of American Nativisms, 1860–1925* (New York: Atheneum, 1963).

31. For one critique of the theory, cf. Edward S. Shapiro, "John Higham and Anti-Semitism," in *American Jewish History* (1986) 76.

32. Simon Kuznetz, "Immigration of Russian Jews to the United States: Background and Structure," in *Perspectives in American History* (1975) 9, pp. 115, 122–123.

33. Cf. John Higham, *op. cit.,* p. 135.

34. Cf. Jonathan D. Sarna, "The 'Mythical Jew' and the 'Jew Next Door,' " in *op. cit.,* p. 59.

35. Morton Borden, *Jews, Turks, and Infidels* (Chapel Hill: University of North Carolina Press, 1984), pp. 101–103.

36. Alexis de Tocqueville, *Democracy in America,* George Lawrence, trans., J. P. Mayer, ed. (Garden City: Doubleday-Anchor, 1969), p. 292.

37. Robert T. Handy, *A Christian America: Protestant Hopes and Historical Realities* (New York: Oxford University Press, 1971), p. 215.

38. Cf. Leonard Dinnerstein and Mary Dale Palsson, eds., *Jews in the South* (Baton Rouge: Louisiana State University Press, 1973), p. 18.

39. Leonard Dinnerstein, *The Leo Frank Case* (New York: Columbia University Press, 1968), pp. 32–33.

40. *Ibid.,* p. 149.

41. See books by Arnold Forster and Benjamin R. Epstein, among them, *The New Anti-Semitism* (New York: McGraw-Hill, 1974).

42. Cf. Leonard Dinnerstein, *op. cit.*, p. 157.

43. William A. Nawyn, *American Protestantism's Response to Germany's Jews and Refugees, 1933–1941* (Ann Arbor: University of Michigan Press, 1981), p. 195. Cf. also Arthur D. Morse, *While Six Million Died: A Chronicle of American Apathy* (New York: Random House, 1967).

44. Editorial, in *The Christian Century,* November 21, 1984, pp. 1093–1094.

45. Cf. Leonard Dinnerstein, "The Origins of Black Anti-Semitism in America," in *American Jewish Archives* (1986) 38:2, p. 113.

46. Cf. Merrill Simon, *Jerry Falwell and the Jews* (Middle Village: Jonathan David, 1984), p. 23.

47. King rightly pointed out a major difference in the two situations: Jewish institutions were not destroyed by antisemitism, but slavery shattered almost every black institution. Cf. James M. Washington, ed., *A Testament of Hope: The Essential Writings of Martin Luther King, Jr.* (San Francisco: Harper & Row, 1986), p. 311.

VI. The Twentieth Century: A Time of Extremes

As we have seen, Christian attitudes about Judaism and Jews have swung widely between contempt and toleration. This ambivalence has been rooted to some degree in antisemitism's arising in unstable popular culture. But more significantly, it is due to Christianity's ancient tensions about its identity in comparison with the older-brother faith that provided all its founders, much of its scripture, and many of its beliefs but that still refused to capitulate to the new message.

Ambivalence is inherent in the relationship. When this ambivalence has been denied, as by St. John Chrysostom and Martin Luther, there has been persecution of Jews and a defensive narrowing of the Christian message to only those beliefs that serve as debating points against the other faith. But when this ambivalence has been acknowledged and addressed by theologians such as St. Paul, John Calvin, and (recently) the Roman Catholic Rosemary Ruether and the Episcopalian Paul van Buren, there has been not only tolerance of Jews but a confident, full opening up of Christianity to what Ruether, in *Faith and Fratricide*, has called "the healing and liberating word that I have heard emerge from the Christian tradition, once freed of its distorted consciousness."

The extremes of the relationship have been reached during the twentieth century. Think about it: within the lifetime of a middle-aged man or woman of 1991 there have occurred the horror of the Nazi final solution (the clear warnings of which most Christians refused to heed and do anything about) and the creation of a Jewish state *and* a vigorous attempt by Christians and Jews to bring tolerance and understanding to Jewish-Christian relations.

The seeds of these events were sown one hundred years ago, at the end of the nineteenth century.

1. THE DREYFUS AFFAIR

We begin with a court-martial that shook the world. In 1894, at the very end of the century of emancipation of the European Jews, a French Army colonel named Henry went to the Paris newspaper *La Libre Parole* with the news that one Captain Alfred Dreyfus had betrayed France by selling military secrets to Germany. It was bad enough that a member of the French general staff was accused of treason. What made the matter of utmost significance was the fact that Captain Dreyfus was a Jew.

The editor of *La Libre Parole* was a notorious Jew-baiting publicist named Edouard Drumont who, using antisemitism as his glue, had succeeded in bonding together in his readership a sizeable number of citizens disenchanted with one aspect or another of modern life. Drumont and other antisemites cleverly made the Jew into the image of a universal villain that handily satisfied the various needs of many disaffected Frenchmen searching for a scapegoat on whom to pin the blame for such contemporary ills as military powerlessness, a sluggish economy, and flagging patriotism.

And so the headline in *La Libre Parole* ran, "Jewish Traitor Under Arrest." Pressed by the resulting popular uproar, the army convicted Dreyfus and sent him to Devil's Island. The sole "proof" was an unsigned note said to be in his handwriting. There was no other evidence. Neither was there any hint of disloyalty. Dreyfus was assimilated, wealthy, secure, and so punctilious that the writer Anatole France concluded that had Dreyfus been one of the prosecutors, "he would have condemned himself."[1] There was, then, no hint of a motive for betrayal. The issue was his Jewishness. "All Jews are guilty," declared the handwriting expert who testified at the first trial, and the writer Maurice Barrés said that all the evidence that he needed to be sure of Dreyfus' guilt was to know his race. Crowds gathered at the Place de la Concorde to shout "Death to the Jew!" Claims in Dreyfus' defense were popularly ascribed to the bribes of a syndicate of wealthy Jews supposedly financing a coverup of Dreyfus' crimes. The public spirit was accurately summarized by Drumont when he said that the issue was not one individual's crime but the shame of an entire race.[2] On January 5, 1895, Dreyfus was put through the humiliation of being publicly stripped of his military insignia, having his sword broken, and paraded before a line of officers who screamed "Judas" in his face. As he was led away in handcuffs, Dreyfus shouted to a group of journalists, "You will tell all France that I am innocent."[3]

In 1896 strong evidence that the note was forged was presented to an army court. The court dismissed the claim in minutes. The novelist Emile

Zola thundered his protest against the army in an article titled "*J'Accuse*" ("I accuse"). Charged with libel, Zola fled the country. But in 1898 Colonel Henry confessed that he had used forged documents in the case, and the next day he committed suicide. At the rehearing, Dreyfus was once again found guilty, although he was soon pardoned by the French president. The wounds of the Dreyfus affair—the most famous case concerning Jewish guilt other than the traditional Christ-killer charges—died slowly. Not until 1906 was the verdict legally overruled.

2. THE BEGINNINGS OF ZIONISM

One of the journalists who heard Dreyfus' plea for exculpation on that January day was Theodor Herzl (1860–1904), an assimilated Hungarian Jew who, trained as a lawyer, had become a professional writer. Though he was at first convinced of Dreyfus' guilt, Herzl came to believe in his innocence. More significant for history, Herzl saw that the affair was only the latest of several serious warnings that the safety of Jews in Europe was extremely tenuous, even for those Jews who had followed the enlightenment's instruction to assimilate.

Europe had gone a long time without nasty antisemitism. But the contagion broke out again in the 1880s. Some of it was the dangerous nonsense familiar to anybody who had read a little medieval history. In France Edouard Drumont's ravings about Jewish untrustworthiness had found a large audience. In Prague a Roman Catholic priest and theology professor named Augustus Rohling declared in his book *The Talmud Jew* that the Talmud allowed Jews to sacrifice children at Easter. The ritual murder libel reappeared: trials were held in Hungary and Germany, and in Austria a Roman Catholic priest wrote a pamphlet on ritual murders and left copies at church doors. In Germany Friedrich Nietzsche produced a philosophy of a boundless "superman" who would rise above what he saw as the "slave morality" of Christianity and Judaism.

Similar trains of thought led to pagan racial dogmas. The idea of "race" was a new and exciting discovery. If people's behavior, talents, and faults could be accurately predicted by comparing head shapes and sizes, as the French amateur scientist Comte de Gobineau promised while he ran around Europe measuring skulls, then there was no limit to the efficient human utilization of biological determinism. Gobineau was able to prove to the satisfaction of many that the most shapely and intelligent heads sat on the shoulders of Nordic racial types. With this evidence to back them up, racial theorists were able to confirm their intuition that there was such a thing as a "pure Aryan race" destined to rule humanity. Of course this idea was groundless. While archeologists know of an Aryan tribe that swept from Russia into the Indian subcontinent in about 1500 B.C.E., and while linguists speak of an Aryan language group, there is no such thing as an "Aryan race," pure or impure. If it was groundless, it was also dangerous. After this pseudo-scientific claim for Teutonic superiority surfaced in Germany in the 1890s in the librettos of the operas of Richard Wagner and the writings of Wagner's son-in-law, the Anglo-German racist Houston Stewart Chamberlain, the myth of the "Aryan race" was accepted as a fact of racial destiny by many non-Jews in Europe and Britain.

More troubling yet were signs that Jew-baiting was becoming political to the point of state policy. In Russia, Czar Alexander III's government began the terrible pogroms in 1881. In the recently united country of Germany, nationalism was heavily flavored by an antisemitism inspired in part by the Protestant chaplain to the Kaiser, Adolf Stoecker, who dedicated his Christian Social Worker's Party to fighting Jewish "domination of German life." One German national battle cry went, "Without Judas, Hapsburg, Rome, / Let us build the German dome." In 1881 three hundred thousand Germans signed a petition urging restrictions on Jews. Although several prominent Germans came out against the petition, the great historian Heinrich von Treitschke put into writing the appalling aphorism, "The Jews are our misfortune."[4]

German antisemitism entered electoral politics in 1887 when one Otto Böckel, whose slogan was "Liberate yourself from the Jewish middleman," was elected to the German Reichstag. Three years later, Böckel formed the antisemitic People's Party, whose platform was the repeal of Jewish emancipation, and the party won five seats in a local election. In 1892 a Jew-baiting pamphleteer named Hermann Ahlwardt joined Böckel in the Reichstag, where parliamentary immunity protected him from prosecution for the vicious libels he was circulating—among them, that Jews were "beasts of prey" that must be exterminated. Not only was Ahlwardt consistently reelected, but antisemitic parties won 263,000 votes in the 1893 German elections. In that same year the blatantly antisemitic Christian Social Party was formed in Austria.[5]

Theodor Herzl, then, had reason to fear for the physical safety of Jews well before the Dreyfus affair. He was willing to try to do something about it, but the means that he chose at first were not very productive. He wrote novels and plays, and considered urging the pope to protect Jews in exchange for a mass conversion. Two events early in 1895—the Dreyfus verdict and the Austrian Christian Socialist Party's clean sweep of Vienna's municipal elections—shocked him back to reality. In April 1895 he decided to become a political activist for Jewish emigration from a society that, day by day, was becoming increasingly threatening. He wrote a pamphlet called *The Jewish State* that declared: "We are a *people, one* people. We have everywhere tried honestly to integrate with the national communities surrounding us and to retain only our faith. We are not permitted to do so." The Jews, "denounced as strangers," would be satisfied to be left in peace by the Gentiles. But, Herzl concluded, "I do not think they will."[6]

Taking every advantage of his charismatic personality and dramatic and fiery appearance, Herzl became the leader of the international Zionist movement. In many areas he was regarded as much more than a political leader, for as a boy living in a *shtetl* (Russian village), David Ben-Gurion, the future prime minister of Israel, heard great things about the Hungarian doctor of law: "A rumor spread that the Messiah had arrived—a tall handsome man—a 'doctor' no less—Dr. Herzl."[7]

But not all Jews welcomed the idea of repatriation. Successful, assimilated Jews believed that Herzl exaggerated the danger, and that one could be both a Jew and a European. Some Orthodox Jews refused to return to Israel until the true messiah came. Many Jews feared that trumpeting about emigration would only inspire the antisemites to greater persecutions. In meeting after meeting of the International Congress of Zionists, in trip after trip to visit heads of state who might support him, Herzl pushed for a Jewish state. In 1903, the year before his untimely death, he even met personally with Pope Pius X. The pope patiently heard Herzl's request for help and responded, "If you come to Palestine and settle your people there, we shall have churches and priests ready to baptize all of you." Herzl himself had had the same idea ten years earlier, but it had lost its appeal.[8]

The most substantial support came from the British government. First it offered to help the Jews settle in the highlands of east Africa, now part of Kenya. Herzl agreed that it might be a temporary refuge for Russian Jews, but other Zionists convinced him that the goal was Mount Zion itself: Palestine and Jerusalem.

This dispute highlights a split in Zionism. There were two factions, labeled "secular" and "religious," emphasizing different aspects of the purpose for leaving Europe. The former stressed, with Herzl, that the goal was to protect Jewish lives. The latter stressed theological reasons for returning to the land that was promised Abraham: the return would establish in *Eretz Israel* ("the land of Israel") a spiritual center for Jews who for hundreds of generations had been wandering in the diaspora. The spokesman for the religionists was a Russian Jew named Asher Ginsberg (1856–1927), who wrote under the Hebrew pen name Ahad Ha'am ("one of the people"). Herzl spoke legalistically of negotiations for geographical territories. He and the other secularists said that Jews formed a nation and, therefore, as a nation had the right to their own land, and that land was Israel. Although Jews had been forced to leave the land, the bond between the people and the land had never been severed. Jews had always wished to return, and the fact that no other nation had taken exclusive possession of this land was proof that it was still theirs. They had an historic right to build their secular nationhood there.

Ginsberg, on the other hand, spoke mystically of a spiritual bond with the land. If there was a right, it was not national and secular but rather historic and spiritual. The relationship between Jews and Israel, he wrote, was unique in history:

> We look unto Zion, and only unto Zion, not as a matter of free choice, but out of natural necessity. For we believe with perfect faith that only there, by force of the historic passion that binds the people to its land, shall our spirit be strengthened and purified, and all of our inner powers be stirred into life. Only thus shall we be able to overcome the tremendous obstacles that stand in the way of a national undertaking of this nature, one which sets out to affect a fundamental transformation in the way of life and the psychology of a people uprooted thousands of years ago from its soil, and accustomed for generations to humbling itself before strangers and enslaving its spirit to them.[9]

A point of contention between the highly westernized lawyer Herzl and the very traditional but, in his own way, equally well-educated Ginsberg was the role that the Hebrew language should play in *eretz Israel*. To Herzl, who was fluent in the modern European languages, Hebrew was not important—better to speak in German and French to convince the Gentiles that Jews were not racially inferior. But to Ginsberg, Hebrew was the whole point. For centuries the Christian churches of eastern Europe had been trying to drive Judaism out of existence; what better proof could there be of the viability of Judaism than to revive Hebrew? Aware that the ancient language of the scriptures had nearly died out among all but the scholars, Ginsberg inspired an entire school of Hebrew-writing poets and religious thinkers. While this division between the children of the enlight-enment and the children of the shtetls—the secularists and the religious ones—has never ended, the fact that Hebrew is now spoken again in daily transactions in Jerusalem suggests the strength of the religious argument. The territory on which the Zionists placed their hopes and labors was owned by Turkey, which, except for a brief period during the crusades, had controlled it since the seventh century. Jews had never stopped living there. Crusaders and Arabs came, but the land was never densely settled, and it had not had an independent political identity for centuries. After 1905 Jews fleeing from Russia began to move there against the increas-ingly violent protests of Arab residents, which soon led to Turkish restric-tions on Jewish immigration to Palestine.

When Turkey allied itself with Germany in 1914, the future of Zion-ism became clearly entangled with the results of World War I. On No-vember 2, 1917, on the eve of Britain's conquest of Palestine, the British foreign secretary Arthur James Balfour issued a declaration of his coun-try's support for Zionism, under the condition that the rights of existing residents not be abrogated. The varied reasons for the Balfour Declaration included grand politics—for example, shortening the war by stimulating pro-British feeling among German and American Jews—as well as Bal-four's apparent personal sympathy with Jews. A key figure in the declara-tion was Louis D. Brandeis, a U.S. supreme court justice and a leader of American Zionists, who succeeded in convincing President Woodrow Wilson to support the idea for a National Home for Jews. The Balfour Declaration by no means settled the issue, and neither did the British government, which, taking over the protectorate of Palestine, was split on the National Home issue.

Ironically, the one single event that made Israel a reality was an act of prejudice. In 1924 the new immigration act in the United States all but closed the trans-Atlantic flow of eastern European Jews to America, even as economic crisis in eastern Europe was forcing more and more emigra-tions. "This was one of the decisive events in the history of Zionism, and the prehistory of Israel," observes Conor Cruise O'Brien:

> Had those doors remained open, great numbers of European Jews would have found refuge in America between 1933 and 1941, and also after the Second World War. Immigration to Palestine in the same period would have been likely to be much less; the pressure toward the creation of the State of Israel would have been proportionately lessened; and it is possible that the British might have succeeded in scaling down

the Jewish National Home to some kind of guaranteed enclave within an independent and predominately Arab Palestine.[10]

Between 1882 and 1903, some twenty-five thousand Jews emigrated from Russia for Palestine. Over the next ten years the figure rose to forty thousand, most of them refugees from the pogroms following the aborted revolution of 1905. In Palestine in 1914, there were eighty-five thousand Jews, amounting to twelve percent of the population. But in 1925, the year after the American immigration quotas went into effect, more than thirty-three thousand Jews entered Palestine, and by 1931 there were almost one hundred and seventy-five thousand Jews, making up about nineteen percent of the population.[11]

The greatest migration of them all would come in the next twenty years, for a reason that made Theodor Herzl's worst predictions seem mild.

3. THE HOLOCAUST

"Holocaust," the English word commonly used to describe Nazi Germany's attempt to destroy Jewry, means "burnt offering" or "great or total destruction of life especially by fire." The Hebrew word used to describe the events in central and eastern Europe in 1938–1945—*shoah* —is less specific about the tools of destruction: *shoah* means "annihilation." Although the Jews of Europe were not completely annihilated by the killing machine that ran the extermination camps between December 8, 1941, when the first Jews were gassed at Chelmno, Poland, and April 1945, when the Germans abandoned the camps under the pressure of invading Allied troops, the end result was so appalling that the word is apt. Given another year, it might almost certainly have been accurate.

Before the events called the "final solution" by their initiators, there were almost nine million Jews in continental Europe north of Spain. By 1945, 5,933,900 Jews, two-thirds of European Jewry, had been gassed, shot, hanged, or tortured to death, mostly in the concentration camps. In Germany, Austria, the Baltic countries, and Poland, ninety percent of all Jews were destroyed. Of Polish Jews, three million were killed.[12] Other "aliens," among them gypsies, gays, observant Christians and communists, perished in vast numbers, but the full power of the Nazi killing machine was systematically unleashed almost exclusively at the Jews. Their destruction was the primary goal in the life and career of Adolf

Hitler and many of his assistants. Verily this was, to quote the title of a recent book on the holocaust, "the war against the Jews."

In a country and century commonly regarded as meeting the highest standards of reason, modernity, and culture, how could this catastrophe have occurred? For a hint of an answer, let us hear Wilhelm Niemöller, pastor of a German Protestant church in the 1930s:

> After the war . . . again and again our failure was pointed out to me, often rather overwhelmingly, and then I was assured that nothing like Hitler could ever have risen in the United States. I smiled patiently because I was, and am, of the opinion that "Hitler" waits and lurks everywhere in some form or shape.[13]

Niemöller was suggesting that while it may make us feel better to believe that the events of the holocaust/shoah were acts of derangement by an individual demon or madman named Adolf Hitler, we should not be so quick to claim innocence.

If Hitler was the devil or a lunatic, he had plenty of company. He did not seize power through conspiracy or in a palace coup. Quite the contrary: he was the elected head of one of his country's largest political parties, a party whose platform was blatantly antisemitic. After his National Socialist Party won thirty-three percent of the vote in 1932 and the German government was locked in a stalemate, he was asked by experienced officials to form a new government.[14]

If Hitler was a popular political figure legitimated at least partially by democracy, little that he said was a surprise to anybody who had followed his career. In his fourteen years in politics before being appointed German chancellor in 1933, he had clearly proposed most of the policies that he later implemented. In his speeches and his writings, among which was a book called *Mein Kampf,* he declared himself for all the world to see as an antisemite of the European nationalist-racist variety. Although Hitler's antisemitism bore some semblance to classic theological anti-Judaism, he was not a Christian. Like Friedrich Nietzsche, he rejected traditional religion in favor of a domineering nihilism that seeks meaning only in the individual, here-and-now act, and suspects anything that comes from outside.

We have all experienced that nihilism at one time or another. However, to acknowledge nihilism and struggle with its shadows is far different from giving into it entirely, as Hitler appears to have done. Perhaps his nihilism derived from his early life, when he lived solely by his own wits in a series of unfamiliar, harsh, and loveless environments with little or no family help or affection. As fascinating as such psychological speculations are, they tell us little about why so many millions of Germans and non-Germans became his followers. He and they despised the "aliens" who, he thought, restricted him and Germany by causing the economic and social turmoil in Germany in the difficult days after World War I. The "aliens" included many groups of non Anglo-Saxons, but foremost among them were the one percent of the population who (he said time and time again) betrayed the "fatherland" after the war, during the war, and for years before the war. These people, of course, were the Jews.

It seems clear that Hitler succeeded because he said and did things that were popular, in a manner that appealed to the masses. The fact that he became a successful political figure says as much. So, too, do his antisemitic words and actions, many of which were extremely familiar not only in their contempt for Jews but also in the "modern," "reasonable," and "scientific" tone in which he presented them. Look at a letter that he wrote in 1919, when he was thirty. Jews, he wrote, are the source of a "racial tuberculosis of nations." He insisted that his views on Judaism were entirely reasonable, consistent, and practical. He said that "rational antisemitism" would produce "a systematic legal opposition" to Jewish privileges. The "final objective" of this carefully thought-out policy "must unswervingly be the removal of the Jews altogether."[15] This combination of racial thought, scientific terminology, nationalism, and appeals to reason was not Adolf Hitler's invention. As we have just seen, it was circulating in Europe before he was born in 1889. At the very time that he was writing this letter, Americans were using very similar arguments to come up with reasons for drastically paring away at Jewish immigration.

To this tried and true formula, Hitler seems to have made two innovations. First, he added to the defensive racism of his day an expectation that, in form, is not unlike the "end-time" anticipations of classic Christianity. Where St. Augustine, Martin Luther, and other theologians believed that the second coming and the end-time would follow on the heels of the conversion of all Jews, Hitler was convinced that Germany would reach its greatest glory only when it was rid of Jews. As he described it in *Mein Kampf,* the "Jewish problem" was postponing Germany's "resurrection."[16] Another way to say this is that his antisemitism was less prophylactic than it was prophetic: contemporary racists wanted to keep Jews away so that "they" would not harm them, while he wanted to remove Jews "altogether" in order to bring on the golden age.

The second innovation followed on the first. Because his ambitions were so grand, he was unusually systematic and aggressive. By patiently and craftily placing himself in a position that allowed him to be called to great power, he was able to work out his agenda in a way that was not solely local and spontaneous. For the first time, antisemitism had become a major policy of state.

Hitler and his followers went to work immediately after he took office as Germany's chancellor. He acted in ways that were entirely consistent with the history of antisemitism, and with the same concern for system and "science" that he showed in his 1919 letter. One of his first steps was to define the racial purity required to be part of the resurrected "Aryan" German state. A "non-Aryan" was defined as someone with at least one Jewish grandparent. On April 1, 1933, two months after he took office, he called for a four-day boycott of Jewish-owned businesses. Then he proceeded to enact some four hundred anti-Jewish laws reminiscent of the Theodosian decrees of the fifth century, as well as of later legislation in Europe and the United States. Laws were passed barring "non-Ayrans" from the legal profession and parts of the medical professions, establishing a five percent quota of Jewish students in public schools, and prohibiting Jews from voting, serving in the government, appearing in motion pictures and plays, and publishing books. After 1935 Jews were no longer allowed to call themselves "Germans." Jewish public speech, newspapers, and even prayers were censored. In short, by 1938 the Jews of Germany were in the same situation that their ancestors had been in before the nineteenth century. They were "disemancipated"[17] by Nazi Germany.

One right still allowed them was emigration, and one hundred and fifty thousand Jews—thirty percent of Germany's Jewish population—emigrated between January 1933 and November 1938. With the United States cut off due to quotas, approximately one-half of the emigrants went to Palestine, whose Jewish population in that period rose to about four hundred thousand or five times what it had been in 1922. This huge influx threatened Arabs, who in 1936 staged a violent revolt that ended only when the British agreed to an immigration quota for Palestine that was one-half the 1935 total and lower than any figure since 1932.[18]

If "disemancipation" pushed the Jews of Germany back into the eighteenth century, the Nazi policies beginning in November 1938 propelled them even further back in time to the middle ages. On November 9–10, 1938, storm troopers were set loose on the Jews in the riot that, because there were so many broken shop windows, came to be called *Kristallnacht* ("night of glass"). Six hundred synagogues were burned, more than seven thousand Jewish shops were ransacked, and thirty-five thousand Jews were arrested. Henceforth Jews in Germany and the countries it would soon conquer were required to live under the medieval codes developed in the twelfth century. They were packed into ghettos, forced to wear the yellow star of identification, and subjected to ever harsher restrictions. The flow of emigrants increased, and between *Kristallnacht* and the beginning of World War II in September 1939, another one hundred and fifty thousand Jews left Germany for sanctuary wherever they could find it. The world was still not listening.

One measure of the hopelessness was that most of those who left were the young, who would have been the ones to resist Hitler had there been a chance. By 1939, eighty percent of the country's Jewish population under the age of forty had fled.[19]

4. THE CHURCH'S RESPONSE

If Hitler's message frightened young Jews, it pleased Christians. Two-thirds of Germany's Protestant clergymen backed National Socialist representatives in elections in the summer of 1933.[20] The general lack of resistance showed the power of the Nazi message in finding true believers or, alternatively, in convincing the doubters to refrain from making strong protests. A German aristocrat who would later be executed for plotting against Hitler wrote in 1933, "Soon there will be a proverb—spineless like a German government official, godless like a Protestant clergyman, honorless like a Prussian officer."[21] Only about ten percent of the Protestant clergy joined opposition groups.[22] The remainder, "godless" or not, either walked the path of least resistance or actively supported the national-racial ideology.

The second option had already been taken by many Christians. In 1921, when Hitler was a violent street politician, some clergy founded an organization called the League for a German Church. On its agenda was the goal of forming a church that dispensed with what one founder called "all Jewish blurring of the pure teaching of Jesus."[23] These modern-day Marcionites worked to have Hebrew scripture and certain rabbinic-sounding ideas of Paul removed from the canon. Later in the 1920s, some league members began to criticize contemporary university theologians for irrelevant ideas, among which was their obstinate refusal to discover God's revelation in the divinely elect German people and its nationalistic urges. The "relevant" point of view was indicated by a churchman's comment about Hitler's National Socialist Party: "Out of the depth of its nature there comes to us a will which is pointing us to a divine commission."[24]

At the urging of the National Socialists, in June 1932 nationalist churchmen founded the German Christian movement. Their first act was to issue a statement of guiding principles mirroring Nazi opinions on German nationalism and *Volk* ("peoplehood"), and on Judaism. Among the declarations were these xenophobic aphorisms: "We want a vital national church that will express all the spiritual forces of our people. . . . We see in race, folk, and nation orders of existence granted and entrusted to us by God. . . . Faith in Christ does not destroy one's race but deepens and sanctifies it. . . . We also demand that the nation be protected against the unfit and inferior." Inevitably came the issue of the Jews. The ninth principle went:

> As long as the Jews possess the right to citizenship and there is thereby the danger of racial camouflage and bastardization, we repudiate a mission to the Jews in Germany. Holy Scripture is also able to speak about a holy wrath and a refusal of love. In particular, marriage between Germans and Jews is to be forbidden.[25]

When they met for their first national synod in 1933, most of the German Christian clergy appeared in jackboots and Nazi party brown shirts.

These simplifications were immediately attacked as idolatry, polytheism, and worse. Of the ideology lying behind them, the philosopher Paul Tillich wrote:

> To the extent to which it justifies nationalism and an ideology of blood and race by a doctrine of divine orders of creation, it surrenders its prophetic basis in favor of a new manifest or veiled paganism and betrays its commission to be a witness for the *one* God and the *one* mankind.[26]

In April 1933, Tillich's name was on the first list of teachers banned by the government. Later that year the faculty of Union Theological Seminary in New York invited him to emigrate, and voluntarily took a five percent reduction in pay to cover his salary.

Those few remaining clergy who stood against the Nazis gathered their forces and, in 1934 at Barmen, issued an opposition statement in the classic Protestant form of a confession of faith. Inspired and partially written by the neo-orthodox Swiss theologian Karl Barth, the Barmen

Confession powerfully attacked as heretical the suggestion that God is revealed not only in scripture but also in the German *Volk*. The confession said nothing explicit to counter the issue of antisemitism because the main goal was to address the fundamental doctrinal issue about the locus of divine revelation.

When those few Christians who opposed the "Aryan" regulations spoke up, they usually concerned themselves with the parochial issue of the status of clergy who, under the new laws, had been removed from their pulpits because they were converts from Judaism. An exception was the young theologian Dietrich Bonhoeffer, who publicly opposed the "Aryan" laws on the grounds that "The church has an unconditional obligation towards the victims of any social order, even where those victims do not belong to the Christian community."[27] Bonhoeffer continued to resist the state in other ways. In 1945 he was executed for taking part in a plot against Hitler's life.

Christian individuals and organizations sympathetic to the Nazis attacked the Barmen Confession for being far too negative about what seemed to them the obvious divine revelation in the German *Volk* and its leader. This was chillingly articulated in a German Christian response to the Confession. It sought justification in quotes from Paul's letter to the Romans:

> In this knowledge we as believing Christians thank God our Father that he has given to our people in its time of need the *Führer* as a "pious and faithful sovereign," and that he wants to prepare for us in the National Socialist system of government "good rule," a government with "discipline and honor." Accordingly, we know that we are responsible before God to assist the work of the *Führer* in our calling and in our station in life.[28]

Not right but might was on their side, and at least one confessor was suspended from the pulpit for daring to tell his congregation that Jesus, not the state, was Lord.

Meanwhile, German Roman Catholics, who made up about one-third of the population, were offering some opposition to the Nazis on the issue of control of Sunday schools. Many years after World War II ended, there was a bitter controversy about what the Roman Catholic Church and Pope Pius XII could have done to save more Jews. The conclusion that made the most sense was that while the pope and Roman Catholics, like the German Protestant Church, might have done much in the past to forestall the Nazi contamination, by the 1930s and 1940s it was too late to make a major impact on a force whose destruction could come only in war. Had the churches not identified themselves with the ideology and politics of the Nazis, their life might have been less easy, but their integrity would have been much greater. As it was, the only group left with any integrity were the Jews, and they were to suffer for it.

5. THE FINAL SOLUTION

Kristallnacht brought to German Jew-baiting a new direction—or, to put it in the context of the history of antisemitism, it reverted to an old one. Hitler had hinted at this in a speech in 1920, back at the beginning of his political career. Speaking of an ideal anti-Jewish campaign, he reportedly laid out a two-stage plan: "First we try to carry it out kindly, and then, when that does not work, with ruthless violence."[29] The "ruthless violence" began to become systematic in Germany in 1938, but it did not become murderous until the summer of 1941 when, during the invasion of the Soviet Union, Hitler gave an order for a program that came to be called the "final solution" to the Jewish "problem." As his aide Heinrich Himmler wrote in a memo, "The occupied eastern territories are to become free of Jews."[30]

In racial theory, the idea of physical elimination had long been implicit, but in practice it was hardly new. For several years there had been a secret Nazi "euthanasia" program by killing people considered "racially valueless." After 1938, German hospitals killed an estimated five thousand deformed children and eighty to one hundred thousand mentally retarded or insane adults.[31] When word of the program leaked out to the German populace, there was widespread outrage and the killings ended. The tools of murder that had been developed in the hospitals were soon adapted for use on others who were "racially valueless," and whose deaths were less controversial.

During the summer of 1941 the government of Germany decided and secretly began to plan an act of evil unprecedented in the long, sorry history of human cruelty and sin: the systematic destruction of a particular group of people. Everywhere the German army went—and by late 1942 it occupied or controlled almost all of continental Europe—it dispatched special troops on the sole mission of searching out Jews, who were then transported to six specially-built killing camps in central Europe. In many areas local residents were pleased to help the Nazis round up their Jewish neighbors. Yet there were a few signs of resistance to inhumanity. The Finnish government refused outright to cooperate with the program, and Bulgarians actively sought and found alternatives to deportation. The one story of national heroism came from Denmark: Danish Gentiles (including King Christian X) demonstrated solidarity with the Jews in public by wearing the yellow star, and in private by hiding and eventually smuggling to safety almost the entire Jewish population of eight thousand.

From the far ends of the Nazi empire Jews were carried to their slaughter. Forced to Auschwitz were eight hundred Norwegians and sixty thousand Greeks, respectively one-half and three-quarters the pre-war Jewish populations. To Belzek were taken the Jews of Lublin, Poland; to Treblinka were forced the Jews of the Warsaw ghetto, or at least the three hundred thousand survivors of the Jewish uprising there. To Sobibor and Mauthausen were dragged one hundred and ten thousand Dutch Jews, three-quarters of the Jewish population of the Netherlands. To Birkenau were pushed Italians. Sometimes the Germans became impatient and did the job in the field: more than one million Soviet Jews were killed near their ghettos and villages.[32]

The rounding-up, transporting, housing, and killing of Jews soon required an enormous logistical apparatus. With this system came an affectless, technical language that drained all humanity from life-and-death events. The denial bordered on madness. When Jews were herded from their ghettos into boxcars, they were "resettled" or "evacuated eastward."

Accounts of this life-in-death—for example, in Claude Lanzmann's film *Shoah* and Elie Wiesel's *Night* and other books—describe a dark world where evil is routinized into perpetual motion. Other than the suffering of the captives, there is no human or moral context to anything that went on in the extermination camps. It is nihilism run wild when "infirmary" means a killing field and ovens are used not to provide sustenance but to destroy the evidence of slaughter. And what is to be made of the guards' self-defeating determination at the end of the war to drag their captives with them as they fled from advancing Soviet troops? Could it be that the Nazis were once again hiding evidence in fear of being found out? Or was it that the hearty, muscular, bullying Nazi identity survived only as long as the last malnourished, shivering, debased Jew was within sight?

6. THE NATIONAL HOMELAND

Among their wartime enemies, the Nazis' cruelty was common knowledge, as was the existence of the camps (there remains some question as to whether the Allies could have done more to halt the flow of the condemned to their gates). The sight that greeted the Allied liberators of the annihilation camps was transforming for Jew and Gentile alike in dramatic ways that gradually came to affect Jewish-Christian relations.

For Jews, the idea of a Jewish state took on the greatest urgency. Out of a period of bitter struggle on three fronts—the field of battle, the field of diplomacy, and the field of Zionist internal politics—the modern state of Israel was formed in 1948. Jews now had control over their own political entity for the first time since the Romans seized Jerusalem in 63 B.C.E. Israel's short history has since seen triumph (in the defense of its existence in the 1967 Six Day War), near-disaster (in the 1973 Yom Kippur War), and extreme controversy (in the 1982 invasion of Lebanon and its aftermath). It has also seen a steady barrage of propaganda and military operations by Arab guerrilla forces and the uprisings of Palestinians. It has seen disagreements among Jews on such issues as geographical expansion, relations with the Arabs, and the role of religion in Israeli life.

The problems in *eretz Israel* are joined by problems outside the land. As always, many Jews worry about the attitudes of the Gentiles, whose incomprehension of and volatility about fundamental Jewish concerns are a matter of historical record. Before, the issue was the legitimacy of the Jews as a particular group with their own distinct customs and religious practices. That issue has not died, but it has been joined and at times supplanted by the question of the legitimacy of the state of Israel itself. Most Jews deeply believe that for sound legal, political, or theological reasons Israel's national independent existence is beyond question, and that the Jewish state is not only right for Jews but also right for the world. Abraham Joshua Heschel hinted at this rightness when he wrote, "Israel is a personal challenge, a personal religious issue. It is a call to every one of us as an individual, a call which one cannot answer vicariously. It is at the same time a message of meaning, a way of dealing with the monsters of absurdity, a hope for a new appreciation of being human."[33]

This message may be obvious to many Jews, but around them they observe the Gentiles wavering. Honest criticism of Israeli policies is often interspersed with the doctrinaire anti-Zionism that the historian Bernard Lewis calls "the new antisemitism." What infuriates Jews is that many Christians do not seem to know the difference between criticism and attack, between sympathy with Arabs and hate for Jews. Therefore, a Christian who wishes to engage in serious dialogue with a Jew must work to identify and separate out these two attitudes. To help tell them apart, Bernard Lewis suggests this rule of thumb:

One of the characteristics of the anti-Jew as distinct from the pro-Arab is that he shows no other sign of interest in the Arabs or sympathy for them, apart from their conflict with the Jews. He is completely unmoved by wrongs suffered by the Arabs, even Palestinians, under any but Jewish auspices, whether by their own rulers or by third parties.[34]

Lewis goes on to say that the anti-Jew (as against the pro-Arab) can be recognized by an exaggerated worry about whether Jews are unduly powerful and influential, and by concerns about the patriotism of the Jews. "The anti-Jew normally proceeds on the assumptions that: (a) the Jews in his country are all rich and clever, (b) they are all working for Israel, and (c) they are committing some offense in doing so."[35]

Only in name does the new antisemitism differ from the old variety.

7. THE DIALOGUE

For many Christians the impact of the discovery of the holocaust's extent led to a transformation of attitudes about Jews and Judaism. In Germany, as clergy who had supported Hitler were being hauled before denazification panels, survivors of the German Confessing Church published a corporate statement of guilt for the part they had played in the crimes of Nazi Germany. Three years later the World Council of Churches confessed, "We have failed to fight with all our strength the age-old disorder which antisemitism represents. The churches in the past have helped to foster an image of the Jews as the sole enemies of Christ which has contributed to antisemitism in the secular world."[36] In 1961 the W.C.C. declared its opposition to the ancient deicide libel. In the following years Jewish and Christian clergy exchanged pulpits, formed local and national inter-faith associations, and took the first steps toward sincere and often admiring evaluations of each other's traditions. Martin Buber, in a critique of Pauline influences on Christianity published in 1951, declared, "From my youth onwards I have found in Jesus my great brother."[37]

Stimulating the conversation was activity by a number of Jewish survivors of Nazi persecution who refused to allow the world to forget the terrible events that had only recently occurred. Perhaps the most valuable of these witnesses was Jules Isaac, an historian who had served as French minister of education and who, during the German occupation, lost his family and nearly his own life to the Nazi killing machine. He devoted the remainder of his days to discovering and publicizing the causes of antisemitism. In 1960, during a brief audience at the Vatican, Isaac convinced Pope John XXIII of the importance of the issue. It was placed on the agenda of the Second Vatican Council. This was not the first demonstration of Roman Catholic concern after the war. In 1949 Pope Pius XII changed vernacular translations of the Good Friday phrase *pro perfidis Judaeis;* Jews were now described as "unbelieving" rather than by the more pejorative and incorrect translation, "perfidious." Ten years later John XXIII eliminated the phrase altogether from the service.

But the watershed event was the Vatican II debate in the early 1960s and its resulting document, *Nostra Aetate,* which brought the issue of Christian attitudes about Judaism to a new level of serious public awareness. This occurred despite intense pressure from Catholic conservatives, Arabs, and Orthodox Christian representatives who for theological and political reasons feared any change in the church's official attitude toward Jews and Israel. Augustin Cardinal Bea and others who sympathized with a shift in church policy succeeded on October 28, 1965, in winning the council's approval of a statement favorable to toleration. The statement is contained in Section IV of the council's Declaration on the Relation of the Church to Non-Christian Religions.

The statement "commends mutual understanding and esteem" between Christians and Jews, rejects antisemitism, and specifically states that God has neither rejected nor cursed the Jews. Most important, the statement proclaims that guilt for the crucifixion of Jesus "cannot be charged against all the Jews, without distinction, then alive, nor against the Jews of today." Many concerned with the issue would have much preferred that "deicide" or some other traditional term be used in this sentence, but compromises had to be made in order to win the council's approval.

While many Jews were encouraged by these developments, some were suspicious. History seemed to provide little reason to trust Christians' good intentions. What was needed was action.

Toleration did not spring up overnight in the Roman Catholic or any other church. *Nostra Aetate* inspired many Christians to reexamine their beliefs and traditions and to act on them. Parishes and denominations, advised at times by Jewish consultants established committees to guide them in an improved portrayal of Jews. Sunday school teaching aids were rewritten, catechisms were changed, courses on Judaism were taught in parochial schools, and seminary curricula were examined.

One example of this development is the foundation in 1986 of the Center for Jewish-Christian Studies and Relations at the General Theological Seminary in New York, a seminary of the Episcopal Church. The stated purpose of the Center is to serve as a concrete embodiment of Christian commitment to further Jewish-Christian relations. It works closely with Hebrew Union College.

The literature on the Jewish-Christian encounter has grown considerably, as shown in the extensive, annotated bibliography by Eugene Fisher in *In Our Time*.[38]

In Appendix I will be found an introduction to the Jewish foundation of Christian worship. It may serve as discussion guide for a practical application of an encounter between Christians and Jews.

Appendix II consists of a brief list of some documents published by various church bodies in efforts to lead to a better theological and experiential understanding of Jews and Judaism.

NOTES

1. Cf. Amos Elon, *Herzl* (New York: Holt, Rinehart & Winston, 1975), p. 127.

2. Cf. Malcolm Hay, *The Roots of Christian Anti-Semitism* (New York: Freedom Library–ADL, 1981), pp. 194, 196–197.

3. Amos Elon, *op. cit.,* p. 128.

4. Cf. Edward H. Flannery, *The Anguish of the Jews: Twenty-Three Centuries of Antisemitism* (New York/Mahwah: Paulist Press, A Stimulus Book, 1985[2]), p. 181.

5. Amos Elon, *op. cit.,* p. 72.

6. *Ibid.,* p. 174 (emphasis in original).

7. Cf. Conor Cruise O'Brien, *The Siege: The Saga of Israel and Zionism* (New York: Simon & Schuster, 1986), p. 74.

8. *Ibid.,* p. 104.

9. Cf. Eliezer Schweid, *The Land of Israel: National Home or Land of Destiny,* Deborah Greniman, trans. (Rutherford: Herzl Press, 1985), p. 112.

10. Conor Cruise O'Brien, *op. cit.,* p. 170.

11. *Ibid.,* pp. 107–108.

12. Lucy S. Dawidowicz, *The War Against the Jews* (New York: Bantam, 1986[2]), p. 403.

13. William Niemoller, "Niemoller Archives," in Franklin H. Littell and Hubert G. Locke, eds., *The German Church Struggle and the Holocaust* (Detroit: Wayne State University Press, 1974), p. 54.

14. Lucy S. Dawidowicz, *op. cit.,* p. 48.

15. *Ibid.,* p. 17.

16. *Ibid.,* p. 18.

17. *Ibid.,* p. 343.

18. Statistics in *ibid.*, p. 191.

19. *Ibid.*

20. Ferdinand Friedensburg, "On Nazism and the Church Struggle," in Franklin H. Littell and Hubert G. Locke, eds., *op. cit.*, p. 250.

21. Edwald von Kleist-Schmenzin, quoted by Peter Hoffman, "Problem of Resistance in National Socialist Germany," in Franklin H. Littell and Hubert G. Locke, eds., *op. cit.*, p. 99.

22. Williston Walker, *et al.*, *A History of the Christian Church* (New York: Scribner, 1985²), p. 690.

23. Cf. Arthur C. Cochrane, *The Church's Confession under Hitler* (Pittsburgh: Pickwick, 1976²), p. 75.

24. *Ibid.*, p. 79.

25. *Ibid.*, pp. 222–223.

26. *Ibid.*, p. 80.

27. Cf. Eberhard Bethge, *Dietrich Bonhoeffer: Man of Vision, Man of Courage* (New York: Harper & Row, 1979), p. 208.

28. Cf. Robert P. Ericksen, *Theologians under Hitler* (New Haven: Yale University Press, 1985), p. 87. The quotes are from Romans 13.

29. Lucy S. Dawidowicz, *op. cit.*, p. 129.

30. *Ibid.*

31. *Ibid.*, pp. 132–134.

32. *Ibid.*, pp. 357–403.

33. Abraham J. Heschel, *Israel: An Echo of Eternity* (New York: Farrar, Straus & Giroux, 1968), p. 225.

34. Bernard Lewis, *Semites and Anti-Semites* (New York: Norton, 1986), pp. 249, 251.

35. *Ibid.*

36. Cf. Arthur Gilbert, *The Vatican Council and the Jews* (Cleveland: World, 1968), p. 3.

37. Martin Buber, *Two Types of Faith* (New York: Macmillan, 1951), p. 12.

38. Eugene Fisher and Leon Klenicki, *In Our Time* (New York/Mahwah: Paulist Press, A Stimulus Book, 1990).

Appendix I:
Jewish Foundations of
Christian Worship

In her book on liturgy, the Anglican writer Evelyn Underhill writes, "Some knowledge and sympathetic understanding of Jewish worship, its awed recognition of One God, and the deep and tender piety of its saints, is essential to any real understanding of Christian worship."[1]

1. JUDAISM'S "THREE-LEGGED STOOL"

Some form of liturgy has been a necessary ingredient of Judaism since its beginnings. According to Jewish tradition, in the third century B.C.E. the high priest Simon I (called Simon the Just) said that Judaism had three fundamental tenets without which it could not survive.[2] Here is how his teaching is described in the Talmud, the commentary on the Torah:

> Simon the Just said: "Upon three things the world is based: Upon the Torah, upon the Temple service, and upon the doing of loving deeds." As regards the third it is said, "I desire love and not sacrifice" [Hosea 6:6]. The world at the beginning was created only by love, as it is said, "The world is built by love" [from Psalm 89:2].[3]

Sacrifice in the Jerusalem temple, observance of the Torah, acts of charity —that was the foundation of Judaism. The term "three-legged stool" has been used to describe them; the whole would topple if any one leg were missing. Before we look closely at the first of these legs, temple sacrifice, let us say a word or two about the other two legs.

Leg 1: The Torah

Torah is often translated "law" (as in "statute"), but it means something closer to "teaching" (as in "tradition"). The books of Genesis, Exodus, Leviticus, Numbers, and Deuteronomy make up the first part of Hebrew scripture, in which the ancient patriarchs establish the traditions, customs, and laws that have guided Jewish life for almost three thousand years. These five books were based on stories, customs, and laws that arose from the collective life of the Israelites from the time of Abraham (about 1800 B.C.E.) to the seventh century B.C.E. At first these traditions were stored in memory and transmitted orally, but eventually they were written down and ascribed to Moses, the great prophet, warrior, and lawgiver who led the Israelites in the great liberating event in Jewish history— the exodus from Egypt to the promised land of Canaan in about 1200 B.C.E. They were eventually written down and, sometime between 500 and 400 B.C.E. the scrolls were collected by a priest named Ezra to form the Jewish canon, or fundamental body of scripture. The two other parts of the Hebrew scripture, the prophets and the writings, were added much later. In the Jewish Bible there are a total of twenty-four books, which include the same material that lies in the thirty-nine books of the Protestant "Old Testament." (The Jewish canon counts as one book each 1 and 2 Kings, 1 and 2 Chronicles, 1 and 2 Samuel, Ezra-Nehemiah, and the twelve minor prophets. The Roman Catholic Bible includes seven additional books, which other Christians place in the Apocrypha.)

Over the succeeding centuries after the Torah was written down, its teachings underwent oral interpretation in order to draw out their relevance for contemporary Jews. Between about 200 and 500 C.E., oral interpretation was edited and written down in three massive collections called the Mishnah, the Palestinian Talmud, and the Babylonian Talmud, which are still carefully studied by scholars and rabbis. A Jew who "knows Talmud" can recite from memory laws and customs that pertain to almost every aspect of Jewish life.

Jewish law differs greatly from church canon law, which applies specifically to the life and organization of churches. The Torah and its interpretations, written down by the rabbis in the Mishnah and Talmud, apply to all of Jewish life. This is because to be Jewish is to live a certain way before God, not to hold to a specific creed or confession. Many laws in the Torah range far and wide into daily life. For example, male Jews are to be circumcised (Gen 17), certain foods are not proper (kosher) to eat, and those that are proper must be prepared in a certain way (Gen 9; Lev 11, Deut 14). Other laws describe ritual cleanliness and uncleanliness (Lev 11–15; Deut 13–14), establish ways for atoning for sin (Lev 16), and ban certain forms of behavior, such as incest and idolatry (Lev 18–19).

Holy Days. There also are laws concerning worship. A priesthood was established to supervise the cult (Ex 28–29), and holy days were specified. The most important of these days were and still are Rosh ha-Shana (new year's day) and, ten days later, Yom Kippur (the day of atonement), when Jews fast and pray for forgiveness of all sins committed during the previous year. On this day, according to the Torah, the chief priest Aaron was to whisper the sins of the Israelites to a goat, which was then let loose in the wilderness (Lev 16). Other feast days required by the law commemorate important seasons and harvests—for example, Shavuot ("weeks") came at the time of the wheat harvest in June, and Sukkoth ("booths," also called the Feast of Tabernacles) celebrated the end of the fall harvest (Ex 23:16). *Pesach* (Passover) was a seven-day festival that celebrated the barley harvest and, more importantly, the great liberating event in Jewish history—the exodus (Ex 12:1–20).

Passover opens with a ritual evening meal called the seder whose ceremonials are guided by a book called the Haggadah, in which the story of the ancient Jews' liberation is told between blessings over wine and bread (according to the Torah, the bread must be unleavened). The Torah itself is so important that in the middle ages Jews created a festival celebrating the law called Simchat Torah ("rejoicing of the Torah"): on the day when the last portion of Deuteronomy is read, and before the reading cycle is renewed at Genesis 1:1, the Torah is carried several times around the synagogue.

The Sabbath. And, of course, there is *Shabbat,* the sabbath day, on which, the Torah commands, "you shall rest" (Ex 23:12) because after the creation God rested on that day. Many Jews take this law literally and reserve the entire twenty-four hours from sunset on Friday to sunset on Saturday exclusively for worshiping God, rejoicing in religious community, resting, and studying the Torah, Mishnah, and Talmud. So important is the sabbath that the Mishnah and Talmud include several special sections dedicated to determining what may and may not be done on that day. On the sabbath, strictly observant Jews avoid financial transactions (even to the point of not carrying money in their pockets), and refuse to drive an automobile, answer the telephone, and even switch electric lights on and off, though any of these prohibitions may be violated if a life is at stake.

All these holy days and festivals are part of the Jewish lunar calendar, in which the beginning of the month is keyed to the appearance of the new moon rather than to solar time. The stages of the moon over Israel governed the calendar, and when there are doubts a holiday might be stretched over two days.

Halakha. The general term for the teachings and their interpretations is Halakha. A good translation of this important term is "a way of going and being"; here we will call it "the teaching." Halakha honors the covenant between the Jews and God by serving as a guide that sanctifies almost every step along the path of life, wherever that step is taken—in the synagogue or in the home. In considerable detail Halakha tells Jews what to eat, how to relate to each other and to non-Jews, how to conduct their businesses, and what to do in hundreds of social and private situations. Halakha, in short, sanctifies everyday life of Jews much the way monastic disciplines sanctify the everyday life of cloistered monks and nuns.

The most strict observance of Halakha is practiced by Orthodox Jews who may be set apart from other Jews by their disciplines. Conservative Jews may observe many Halakic laws and customs, and Reform Jews generally observe some or few of them.

To observe the teaching is to declare a special relationship with God that reaches far beyond the house of worship into one's home and family. As Jewish history has shown, this unique identity has often attracted the world's scorn, but at the same time it has sustained one of the few religious faith cultures to survive since ancient times. The key element of this relationship is that it lies with a belief in one single God. When Jesus said that the "first commandment" is to love only one God (Mk 12:29–30), he quoted almost word for word from the magnificent Hebrew declaration of monotheism called *Shema Israel* "Hear, O Israel" (Deut 6:4–5):

> Hear, O Israel: The Lord is our God, the Lord is one; and you shall love the Lord your God with all your heart, and with all your soul, and with all your might.

So important is this statement of faith in the one God that Jews are expected to recite it twice daily. In a world of polytheistic religions dominated by harsh, fearsome gods, this declaration that there is a single loving God was a very radical statement. Perhaps equally radical was the instruction to love God with the heart, which for ancient Jews was the seat of intelligence. To make this point in Greek, the version of the *Shema* in the Christian scriptures adds "and with all your mind."

Leg 2: Acts of Charity

Many Christians believe that the Torah is simply a cold, dry legal system that imposes harsh discipline and punishments for those who cannot toe the line. However, there is plenty of room in the Torah and Halakha for another leg of Simon's stool, the practice of acts of piety, justice, and charity. If the meaning of the ten commandments can be summarized in one word, that word would be "fairness." Jesus' "second commandment," "You shall love your neighbor as yourself" (Mk 12:31), is taken word for word from the Torah: "You shall not take vengeance or bear any grudge against the sons of your own people, but you shall love your neighbor as yourself: I am the Lord" (Lev 19:18).

Other laws in the Torah require hospitality for impoverished relatives and sojourners (Lev 25), specify cities of refuge for people who have unintentionally killed others (Num 35), and establish just weights and measures (Deut 25). Workers must be allowed to eat from their own produce (Deut 25:4), and a newly married couple is allowed to live together for a year before the husband is sent away on business or army duty (Deut 24:5). Strangers are to be protected, "for you were strangers in the land of Egypt" (Ex 23:21). In every seventh (sabbatical) year, in recognition that the land is God's and that human ownership is only temporary, the teaching requires that the fields must be left to lie fallow and that the poor may glean off it (Ex 23:10–11; Ru 2).

Therefore, charitable works, justice, and fairness toward all people are part of the fabric of Jewish tradition. And since many of these deeds are directed by Jews to other Jews, they are an important reason why Jewish culture has survived intact under great duress for all these centuries.

Leg 3: The Temple and Sacrifice

Finally, we come to the third leg of the stool of Simon the Just, which will lead us to a discussion of Jewish liturgical life. This is twice-daily sacrifice of animals that was conducted in the Jerusalem temple.

When we speak of "the temple," we mean two distinct houses of worship that stood on the same plot of ground in Jerusalem, from about 1000 B.C.E. to 70 C.E. Some of the ruins of the temple are visible in Jerusalem today. The temple referred to in the Christian scriptures (for example, in Mk 11 and Mt 19) was the second of these buildings. It was the successor to the great and richly decorated first temple that was built by Solomon, King David's son and successor, in the tenth century B.C.E. (1 Kgs 6), and that was destroyed by the occupying Babylonians in 586 B.C.E. (2 Chr 36) when many Jews were taken into captivity in Babylon. Fifty years later, in 537 B.C.E., Cyrus of Persia conquered Babylon and allowed the Israelites to go home. The returning exiles and Jews who had stayed behind in Jerusalem began construction of the smaller and more modest second temple (see the books of Ezra and Nehemiah). These exiles were the first people to be called "Jews," which referred to their home territory, Judea. For almost six hundred years, until the Romans destroyed it in the Jewish War of 66–73 C.E., the second temple was the liturgical center of Jewish life in Israel.

Sacrifice and Covenant. The central act of worship in both temples was the daily sacrifice, which commemorated the covenants that God made with the Jewish patriarchs during divine revelations. In the covenant God agrees to protect the Jews in exchange for a commitment of loyalty and faithfulness. This dual agreement signifies that a real relationship exists between both parties. Such an agreement is so important that humans seal it with the giving-up of something valuable—a "sacrifice," which is a word derived from the Latin word for "make sacred."

The first covenant in Hebrew scripture was the one between God and Noah in Genesis 8–9. After Noah appealed to God with an especially fragrant sacrifice (Gen 8:20–21; 9:1), God promised Noah, first, that humans henceforth would have dominion over the animals and, second, that the chaotic destruction of the flood would not be repeated. In exchange, Noah and his descendants were to live in justice and must not eat flesh from living animals.

As the rabbis interpreted the covenant in the Babylonian Talmud (Sanhedrin 56A), Noah was expected to observe seven laws of moral conduct. He was prohibited from tolerating a miscarriage of justice, from cursing God, from worshiping idols and planets, from engaging in illicit sexual intercourse (including adultery, sodomy, and incest), from taking life wrongfully, from stealing, and from eating parts severed from a living animal.

Sacrifice also played a part in the two other important covenants in Hebrew scripture, the one with Abraham and the other with Moses. In Genesis 15–17, after Abraham made a sacrifice, God promised that he and his descendants would thrive and settle in "all the land of Canaan." In exchange, they must identify themselves and acknowledge God's protection by circumcising all males. God renewed this covenant with Abraham's grandson Jacob at Bethel. Jacob declared: "Surely the Lord is in this place. . . . This is none other than the house of God," and immediately went about setting up a pillar, or sacrificial table, that "shall be God's house." He poured oil on the altar and promised to make another kind of sacrifice, a tithing (Gen 28). Later, on Mount Sinai God offered Moses and the Jews continued personal protection if they would observe the ten commandments and honor God's name with sacrifice. "In every place where I cause my name to be remembered," God declared, "I will come to you and bless you" (Ex 19:5; 20:24).

Various kinds of animals were sacrificed in the temple, but it was the lamb that was most commonly used. We should say here that the Jewish Bible is contemptuous of the human sacrifices practiced by other Middle Eastern peoples. The Torah prescribed that "two male lambs a year old day by day be continually" offered on the altar, one in the morning and the other in the evening (Ex 29:38–39; Num 28:3–4). "Lamb" and sacrifice became closely identified with each other, as the use of the lamb in the moving "suffering servant" poem of Isaiah 53 testifies. This theme was appropriated by early Christians who identified Jesus as the sacrificed "Lamb of God" (Jn 1:36; Episcopalians and many other Christians use these words in the "Glory to God" canticle that opens the eucharist).

The Psalms. For hundreds of years in the first and second temples, these sacrifices probably took precedence over any other ritual as Jews relived the great covenants of ancestry. But other elements gradually appeared. One was the singing of hymns, called psalms, many of which had been written during the exile of the sixth century B.C.E. The "hymnbook of the second temple," as the book of Psalms has been called, includes several psalms that echo Jacob's belief that God dwells in a specific holy place. For Jacob this place was the pillar at Bethel; for the psalmist, it was the Jerusalem temple itself:

How lovely is thy dwelling place,
O Lord of hosts!
My soul longs, yea, faints
for the courts of the Lord;
My heart and flesh sing for joy
to the living God (Ps 84:1–2).

2. THE FIRST SYNAGOGUES

Around the time that the psalms began to be introduced into the Jerusalem temple, another institution of Jewish worship developed. It lay outside the walls of the temple and did not involve daily sacrifice. This institution eventually took on the Greek name *synagogue,* or "assembly." Some scholars believe that the roots of the synagogue lay in the devastating experience of the Babylonian exile when, forcibly removed far from Jerusalem, the Jews had to create new structures of worship outside the temple. One confirmation of this theory is a vision of the prophet Ezekiel in which he is told by God, "Though I removed them far off among the nations, and though I scattered them among the countries, yet I have been a sanctuary to them for a while in the countries where they have gone" (Ez 12:16).

Whenever and wherever it appeared, the belief that God could be worshiped outside the temple led many Jews to gather together in order to worship not through sacrifice—that could be done only in the temple by priests—but through reading and studying the Torah. In the Jewish tradition, study is often regarded as an act of prayer, although it is expected to go alongside a life of charity, as the following quote from the section of the Talmud called the Mishnah suggests. The quote is attributed to a rabbi who was born in about 80 C.E.:

> Rabbi Elisha ben Abuyah said that a man who has learnt much Torah and has good deeds is like a horse which has reins. The man who has the first, but not the second, is like a horse without reins; it soon throws the rider over its head.[4]

The Beginnings of the Synagogue

A very early, if not the first, service of worship in a synagogue is described in considerable detail in the eighth and ninth chapters of the book of Nehemiah, which was written in about 425 B.C.E. Although this worship service took place in Jerusalem, it was not held inside the rebuilt temple but rather outside in the courtyard. It was led by Ezra. Many modern-day Christians and Jews would feel quite at home in Ezra's service, which had seven characteristics in common with twentieth century services.

1. There were *worship leaders.* "And Nehemiah, who was the governor, and Ezra the priest and scribe, and the Levites who taught the people said to all the people, 'This day is holy to the Lord your God . . .'" (Neh 8:9). In the time of Moses, the tribe of Levi was appointed to serve Aaron, the first priest (Num 3:6–10). Today many services are led by trained people, both ordained and lay; in the Episcopal Church and other religious traditions, they serve in a hierarchy.

2. The worship service was *public, exclusive, and different* from nor-

mal life. "The people of Israel were assembled with fasting and in sackcloth, and with earth upon their heads. . . . The Israelites separated themselves from all foreigners" (Neh 9:1–2). Today, most worship remains distinct from day-to-day secular life, and worshipers usually gather in a building that is very unlike workaday structures, and in groups defined by differences in liturgy and belief.

3. The service provided *a link to the tradition* through scripture reading and study. "They read from the book of the law of the Lord their God" (Neh 9:3). Scripture reading is a vital part of all contemporary worship.

4. The worshipers *acknowledged their own fallibility and God's sovereignty.* "They made confession and worshiped the Lord their God" (Neh 9:3). The regular confession of sins, sacraments of reconciliation, and days of penance are key elements in twentieth century worship services of most faiths.

5. There was a *thanksgiving.* "Then the Levites . . . said, 'Stand up and bless the Lord your God from everlasting to everlasting" (Neh 9:5). God both blesses humans through steadfast love and is blessed *by* them in thanksgiving for divine love and protection. A blessing-thanksgiving appears frequently in *The Book of Common Prayer.*

6. A priest retold *the sacred story* that defined the people's special relationship with God. "And Ezra said . . ." (Neh 9:6–37). For Jews, the sacred story is the one about the exodus.

7. The worshipers *reaffirmed the special relationship.* "Because of all this we make a firm covenant and write it . . ." (Neh 9:38). Where Jews renewed the covenant, today's Christians renew their commitments through the recitation of the Nicene and Apostle's Creeds and in the eucharist.

The first non-temple service led by Nehemiah and Ezra was eventually followed by many other synagogues. By the first century C.E., Jews were meeting in buildings, also called synagogues. To form a synagogue, all there had to be was a group of ten men called a minyan. Whether or not later synagogue services followed all the seven steps of that first service, they had one aspect in common: the Torah was read aloud to the assembly of worshipers, first in Hebrew—the ancient language in which it was written—and then in Aramaic—the common language of the Middle East derived from Hebrew. When they read the Torah aloud, the worshipers in the synagogue commemorated the covenant much the way that the priests did by sacrificing in the temple, and through that commemoration they symbolically reenacted the covenant. Initially in sabbath services, and later daily, Jews everywhere gathered to hear the Torah read.

Scholars have been able to recreate the way the reading was done. First, there was a berakah, or blessing of praise and thanksgiving, for example, "Bless the Lord who is to be praised" (which Christians echo today with the words, "Glory to you, Lord Jesus Christ," before the gospel reading). Then the section of Torah was read in Hebrew. The readings probably followed no set pattern at first, but they eventually ran in an annual or triennial cycle beginning with Genesis 1:1 and ending with the death of Moses at Deuteronomy 34:12. The reader paused after every verse while a translator put it into Aramaic.

At first, scholars believe, only the Torah was read during a synagogue service. Later, readings were added from the other books; the reading from a book of the prophets was called the haftarah ("completion"). These readings came to follow a lectionary (much like the readings assigned in today's church lectionaries) so that the subject matter conformed with the season; for instance, the book of Esther was read at Purim because it concerns the origins of that festival. The synagogue chose their prayer leaders and lectors from among their own number. The Torah reading would be divided between as few as three and as many as seven men, depending on the solemnity of the day.

Following the reading or readings, one or more blessings (similar to the ones that Christians use following readings from scripture) were said, and then a preacher would usually give a sermon based on the text or texts or on some aspect of Jewish tradition. Someone who was especially well educated, and who was referred to as "the sage," might be appointed to this important task on feasts and sabbaths.

Prayers would be said at several points during the service. They depended partly on who was leading the service, although certain prayers were obligatory. The monotheistic creed, the *Shema Israel,* opened the service. At some stage during the service, the ten commandments were recited and some prayers were said. Over time, a set of eighteen standard blessings or benedictions appeared. In all, from *Shema* to the end of the sermon, the sabbath service must have been very long, if we are to believe the saying, "On the sabbath one comes early to the synagogue and leaves late." It was the only service of the week until well into the Common Era, when Friday evening services began to be held.

3. TABLE PRAYERS AND RITUAL WASHINGS

The blessing-thanksgiving theme was not limited to the synagogue. It was echoed in prayers at home and in purification rites involving ritual washings. Since both of these types of worship are integral to Jewish and Christian worship, we should learn a few details about them.

Table Prayers

Given the high value that the Jewish tradition places both on the sanctity of daily life and on community spirit, it is not at all surprising that meals play an important part in liturgical life. Fellowship of family and friends around the life-sustaining elements of God's creation takes on a profound spiritual dimension. Some of these meals are ceremonial: Passover opened with the seder, and on the sabbath there may have been a large community meal for the minyan, where the Torah was discussed. But even everyday family meals were conducted with due regard for their sanctity. In many of these prayers, God was praised and blessed as the king of the universe, thanked for creation, and beseeched for salvation. Blessings were said at the beginning and the end, as well as over the wine and bread. The following prayers to God from a modern day siddur (prayer book) are representative of this tradition. These are prayers said over the table on Friday night:

> Blessed are You, Adonoy our God, Ruler of the Universe, Creator of the fruit of the vine.

> Blessed are You, Adonoy our God, Ruler of the Universe, Who takes bread out of the earth.

The last word was Amen—"so be it."

The Hebrew noun Adonoy means Lord, which is used in place of God's scriptural name, Yahweh. This is the reason why, when Moses asked for God's name during their encounter at the burning bush, God answered, "YHWH." As there were no vowels in ancient Hebrew, scholars have had to guess that the name was pronounced "Yahweh." Jews believed that to say anyone's name was to assert authority over that person. Since God's authority cannot be challenged, God's self-proclaimed name must not be uttered. Therefore Jews referred, and continued to refer, to God using various monarchical terms, such as Lord and king of the universe, instead of the holy name. Many Christian Bibles follow the same policy in their translations of YHWH. "Father" as a term for God is very rare in Hebrew scripture (according to Professor Phyllis Trible of Union Theological Seminary, it is used fewer than two dozen times) but is very prevalent in the Christian scriptures, especially in John's gospel, with its strong emphasis on Jesus' divine Sonship. The familiar word *Abba* ("daddy") is mostly used when Jesus speaks of God.

Incidentally, an excellent example of the significance of the meal in Jewish life is found in its centrality in the ministry of Jesus. In Luke's gospel alone there are six dining scenes at which important discourses take place; in three of them Jesus joins Jewish leaders at the dining table (Lk 7, 11, 14). Several post-resurrection appearances of Jesus take place at meals (Lk 24; Jn 21). And, of course, the event that Christians reenact in the eucharist was a supper (Mt 26; Mk 14; Lk 22); we will soon see how the eucharist developed out of these Jewish table prayers.

Ritual Washings

With the Torah's repeated concern for cleanliness, water played an important ritualistic role as a purifying agent well before Jesus' day. Some of the most specific tracts on the subject of ritual purity repeatedly prescribe a washing in water as purification after exposure to uncleanliness (Lev 11–15). This was not merely personal hygiene: someone who was unclean was not permitted to eat sacred food, read or study the Torah, or even pray. Water had a profound spiritual meaning. When Isaiah had God say, "Wash yourselves; make yourselves clean; remove the evils of your doings from before my eyes" (Is 1:16), he was referring to the cleanliness of souls, not hands. Carrying this two-level idea even further, the psalmist saw water as akin to the Torah itself. Psalm 1 compares the righteous person whose "delight is in the law of the Lord" with a fruitful tree that is "planted by streams of water." And note this beautiful passage from the Mishnah:

> As water is gratis for all, so is the Torah gratis for all. As water is priceless, so is the Torah priceless. As water brings life to the world, so the Torah brings life to the world. As water brings a man out of his uncleanliness, so Torah brings a man from the evil way into the good way.[5]

Generally, it was enough simply to wash one's hands to prepare oneself for worship, but there are some indications that immersion in water may have been practiced. In the apocryphal book of Judith, probably written in the second century B.C.E., the heroine each night bathes in a spring. "When she came up from the spring," we are told, "she prayed to the

Lord God of Israel to direct her way for the raising up of her people. So she returned clean and stayed in the tent until she ate her food toward evening" (Jdt 12:7–9).

The goal of immersion may have been complete cleanliness, as the story of Judith suggests, or there may have been a symbolic significance (for example, the recovery of the baby Moses from the Nile or the salvation of the Jews when the Red Sea collapsed on the pursuing Egyptians). In any case, around the time of Jesus not only did the synagogues have baths as well as basins in which people could wash before worship, but the Jewish Essene sect practiced baptism of converts through immersion in flowing water. Jesus' forerunner, John, was called "the Baptist" for a good reason, for like many wandering preachers in the first century C.E., he prepared people for the coming of the messiah with baptism. A Jewish baptism was completed with a mark on the forehead with the initial "T" (Taw), which as the last letter in the Hebrew alphabet signified God. This letter, scholars believe, branded the convert much the way God put a mark of protection on Cain (Gen 4:15).

4. EARLY CHRISTIAN WORSHIP

Much of what we have said about ancient Jewish worship still holds true in Jewish life today. The Torah reading remains the central event of the synagogue service, and blessing/thanksgiving prayers continue to be said over the bread and cup, much as they have been for well over two thousand years. Let us now look at how these Jewish rites influenced Christian worship, which itself has changed little in almost two thousand years.

Of the early Christian communities we are usually told, first, that they worshiped God in a strikingly new way, and, second, that in order to do so they were forced to hide out from persecutory Jews and cruel Romans in moldy catacombs. While that portrayal makes for misty-eyed Hollywood romance, it is bad history. During the first hundred or so years after Jesus was crucified, Christian groups not only worshiped much the same way that Jews did, but they also went about their religious lives openly. If they had any problems, those were not with the political authorities but rather (as some of Paul's letters and the book of Acts make very clear) with themselves as they bickered about the meaning of the Jesus-story and how that meaning should be acted out in their daily and worshiping lives.

Far from inventing a whole new type of worship, the early Christians considered themselves still Jewish and worshiped as Jews did, that is, in fellowship, both in the temple and in assembly at meals. This should not be surprising, for the first Christians in Palestine—often called "Nazarenes" because their messiah came from Nazareth—were Jews, as was their crucified leader. To pick three examples, the Acts of the Apostles, the scriptural history of the early church, tells us the following:

- The apostles attended the temple daily and had communal meals, "praising God and having favor with all the people" (Acts 2:46).
- Paul participated (and gave a sermon) in a synagogue service at Antioch (Acts 13–14:43).
- The apostles "were all together in one place" on Pentecost, the Jewish commemoration of the giving of the law (Acts 2:1, Lev 23:15–21).

Yet there was one important new ingredient: the Nazarenes added to the ancient stories and teachings of the Torah the much newer account of the death and resurrection of Jesus of Nazareth, with whom some of them had traveled around Galilee and Judea for a year or two. The earliest mention of this story in the New Testament comes in Paul's first letter to the Corinthians, which was written only about twenty years after the events it describes. There Paul called the story a *gospel,* which means "good news" (1 Cor 15:1–5). No doubt this account, like others of Paul's letters, was circulated to many small Christian communities scattered around the Mediterranean Sea to be read aloud at a worship service to encourage believers who were feeling lonely and beleaguered. Due partly to the uniqueness of this story and its import, Jesus-followers by the last third of the first century began to think of themselves as distinct from the Jews, and were beginning to meet apart from the synagogues in an *ekklesia,* another Greek word, meaning assembly. This came about both because they chose to worship separately and because Jews, for various reasons, began to exclude them from the synagogues.

Besides this telling of the Jesus story, what form did the worship of the early Christians take? The two main events in Christian worship, then and now, have been baptism and the eucharist, and both have deep roots in Judaism.

Baptism

The Christians baptized prosletytes, just as the Jewish Essenes and the Jew John the Baptist did (Acts 2:38–41).

Sociologically, baptism was the one rite of admission into the *ekklesia*. Theologically, it was seen as a sanctifying, purifying rite that cleansed converts of sin in preparation for confessing Jesus as Lord (see 1 Cor 6:11). To quote Paul, to be baptized was to come "into Christ" and to "put on Christ" (Gal 3:27). Like the Essene converts, new Christians went through a rigorous period of training before being baptized. The ceremony took place on Easter morning. The baptizers probably made the "T" (Tau) sign, which some interpreted as the sign of the cross, and said special blessings along with it.

Little else is known about baptism in the days of the apostles during the first century. However, more is certain about the second century through a surviving catechism titled "The Teaching of the Twelve Apostles," otherwise known as the *Didache*, a Greek word that, similar to "Torah," means "teaching." Written sometime between 100 and 150, the *Didache* provides detailed instructions about Christian worship.

Baptism, this document tells us, proceeds in three steps. First the converts are instructed in Christian doctrine and ethics. Then they and the baptizer must fast. And finally comes the ritual itself. The author of the Didache prefers the use of cold running water, but he is not adamant; warm water and water poured three times over the convert's head are acceptable. What is more important is the trinitarian baptismal formula that must be recited: "In the name of the Father and of the Son and of the Holy Spirit" (also found in Mt 28:18).

By the mid-first century, the church father Justin Martyr was combining the water imagery of baptism with the image of light when he called baptism an "illumination" of an inner experience of the truth of Jesus Christ.[6] This is only one example—John's gospel is another (see Jn 3)—of the parallel symbolism of light and water to suggest the truth and purity of God's revelation.

The Eucharist

For early Christians (and for an increasing number of Christians today), baptism was the sole qualification for the eucharist, or the celebration of the Lord's supper. The eucharist is the central element of Christianity because it commemorates the great events of the faith: God's coming among us in human form, and Jesus Christ's death and atonement for our sins.

The eucharist owes much to the Jewish tradition. As the ritual's very name (derived from the Greek word for thanksgiving) suggests, it was shaped by the thanksgiving blessings recited in the synagogues and over meals. "The clue to early Christian understanding of the Eucharist," writes the church historian and Episcopal priest Richard Norris, "perhaps lies in the idea and act of thanksgiving itself."[7] The major eucharistic prayer was and still is called The Great Thanksgiving. In it Episcopalians, for example, clearly echo the Jewish heritage in the beautiful description of the eucharist as "our sacrifice of praise and thanksgiving."[8]

The eucharistic thanksgiving prayer borrows directly from the Jewish thanksgiving blessings, and is the Christian equivalent of the Jewish acts commemorating the covenant. Jews give thanks to God through the public reading of the Torah in the synagogue, the blessings over the bread and cup, and the celebration of the festivals recalling the great events in God's covenanted relationship with the people of Israel. Those rituals brought the Jewish community together; they also extended that community back to Moses, Jacob, and Abraham. Using similar symbols and institutions, Christians shared the experience of the crucifixion and resurrection—the great liberating and identifying events of their faith—through the ritualized table fellowship of the eucharist, during which the wine and bread were blessed in thanksgiving for God's gifts. The relevant Greek word is koinonia, which means participation or communion ("ecumenical" is derived from it). In the earliest New Testament mention of the eucharist, Paul asks, "The cup of blessing which we bless, is it not a koinonia in the blood of Christ? The bread which we break, is it not a koinonia in the body of Christ?" (1 Cor 10:16).

Therefore, if the sacrifice was the organizing principle in temple Judaism because it commemorated the covenants, and the Torah reading served the same function in synagogue-Judaism because it commemorated the giving of the law, then the eucharist was the organizing principle in Christianity because it commemorated the life and death of what came to be considered the new covenant and the law in Jesus Christ. No wonder, then, that the Roman Catholic scholar Louis Bouyer (who devoted more than twenty years to a study of the origins of the eucharist) once wrote, "If there is one element in the whole of Christian tradition that in all of the forms in which it is known shows the continuity with and dependence on Judaism, it is the Eucharistic prayer."[9]

In the very early church, the eucharist preceded a community meal of the ekklesia that was called an agape or "love feast." Each was important, but in different ways. In his first letter to Corinth, in which he recites the words of Jesus at the last supper, Paul criticizes the Corinthians for not carefully differentiating the eucharist from the agape. Apparently people were rushing through the eucharist as though it were a regular meal, without reflecting on its spiritual meaning (1 Cor 11:20–33). The eucharist, he wrote, was not just a meal for those whose stomachs were empty; it was vastly more.

The *Didache* tells us that prayers were said over the cup and bread. The prayer of consecration over the wine quoted in the *Didache* has strong elements of Jewish table blessings:

> We thank you, our Father, for the holy vine of David, your child, which you have revealed through Jesus, your child. To you be glory forever.[10]

According to the church father Justin Martyr, a hierarchical element was added to the partaking of what he called "this food we call the eucharist." After the group of Christians prayed and greeted each other with a kiss, "then bread and a cup of water and mixed wine are brought to the president of the brethren." This official then offered up prayers and "thanksgiving at some length that we have been deemed worthy to receive these things" from God. This prayer of thanksgiving consecrated the elements, which were then distributed to the congregation by deacons, who used the words quoted by Paul. According to Justin, another eucharist was held at the Sunday service, after readings from Hebrew scripture and "the memoirs of the apostles" and after a sermon by the president. Sunday was chosen because it was the day of the week on which God began to create the universe and Jesus was resurrected.[11]

NOTES

1. Evelyn Underhill, *Worship* (New York: Crossroad, 1984), p. 194.
2. This may be the Simon described so glowingly in the fiftieth chapter of the apocryphal book of Sirach, also called Ecclesiasticus.
3. Aboth of R. Nathan, IV, IIa, in C.G. Montefiore and H. Loewe, eds., *A Rabbinic Anthology* (New York: Schocken, 1974²), p. 430.
4. *Ibid.,* p. 177.
5. Sifre Deuteronomy, Ekb. 48, f 84a, in *ibid.,* p. 164.
6. Justin Martyr, *First Apology,* in *The Ante-Nicene Fathers,* Cleveland Coxe, ed. (Grand Rapids: Eerdmans, 1981), vol. I, chap. 61.

7. Cf. Williston Walker *et al., A History of the Christian Church* (New York: Scribner, 1985⁴), p. 109.

8. *The Book of Common Prayer,* p. 335.

9. Louis Bouyer, *Liturgical Piety,* pp. 129ff.

10. *The Didache,* in *Early Christian Fathers,* Cyril C. Richardson, trans. and ed., (New York: Macmillan-Collier, 1970), 7:3.

11. Justin Martyr, *op. cit.,* chaps. 65–67.

Appendix II:
Some Recent Christian Documents and Guidelines on Jews and Judaism

I. Guidelines for Catholic-Jewish Relations, 1985. Obtainable from: National Conference of Catholic Bishops, Secretariat for Catholic-Jewish Relations, 3211 Fourth Street, N.E., Washington, D.C. 20017-1194.

II. Ecumenical Considerations on Jewish-Christian Dialogue. World Council of Churches, 1983.

III. The Churches and the Jewish People: Towards a New Understanding. World Council of Churches, 1988.

IV. A Theological Understanding of the Relationship between Christians and Jews. Office of the General Assembly, Presbyterian Church (USA), 1985.

V. Relationship between the United Church of Christ and the Jewish Community.

VI. Guidelines for Christian-Jewish Relations, for Use in the Episcopal Church, 1988.

Documents obtainable from: Office on Christian-Jewish Relations, National Council of the Churches of Christ, 475 Riverside Drive, New York, NY 10115.

Index

Absolutism, pagan, 77
Ahad Ha'am, 108
Akiba, 28
Ambivalence, relationship, 106
Ambrose, 37
    and Jews, 50
    and toleration, 51
American Jewry, 80ff
Americanism, 90
Anti-Defamation League, 99
Anti-Judaism, 6
    theological, 7, 21
Antisemitism, American, 88ff, 95f
    black, 101
    clerical, 64
    polite, 28
    racial, 6
    rational, 115
Anti-Zionism, 96f, 102, 122
Attributes, of God, 31
Augustine, 37
    and Jews, 50
    and toleration, 51

Baal Shem Tov, 69
Badge, distinctive, 63
Baptism, 140f
    forced, 60
Bar Kokhba war, 26, 28
Barmen Confession, 118

Barth, Karl, 118
Blind beggar story, 20
Bonhoeffer, Dietrich, 119
Breslauer, Daniel, 32, 72
Buren, Paul van, 106

Cabbala, 68
Charity, Jewish, 130f
Chaucer, Geoffrey, 63
Christian attitudes to Jews, 123f
Christian Century, 101
Christian history, 5
Christian scriptures, 5
Christian worship, early, 139
Christianity, Jewish context of, 7
Chrysostom, 49
Church, against Jews, 48
Circumcision, 27
Cohen, Gerson D., 85
Colonial legislation, 91
Contempt, rhetoric of, 6, 43
Conversion attempts, 50, 91
    defense against, 92
Cossacks, 65
Covenant, 13, 132
Cowan, Paul, 89
Crusades, 59f

Daily life, sanctification of, 35
Davies, W.D., 13

Deicide, 22, 44, 64
Demonization of Jews, 64
Dialogue, 123f
Diaspora, 29
Discussion, manner of, 35
Disemancipation, 116
Dreyfus affair, 107f

Elders of Zion Protocol, 100
Elvira, Council of, 52
Emancipation, 77f
Emperors and Jews, 53
England, Jews in, 62
Enlightenment, 74f
Eretz Israel, 111
Essenes, 8
Eucharist, 141f
Eusebius, 26, 48

Farakan, Louis, 102
"Final Solution," 120f
Frank, Leo affair, 98

Garb, distinctive, 61
Garrison, William L., 96
Gemara, 34
Ghetto, 61, 65
God, imminence and
    transcendence, 30
Good Friday Prayer, 21, 124
Gospels, goal of, 18
Grace and law, 13
Graetz, Heinrich, 29

Halakha, 16, 130
Handy, Robert T., 97
Hasidim, 9, 68
Hebrew language, 111
Hebrew scriptures and love, 13
Hebrew Union College, 83

Hegesippus, 47f
Hertzberg, Arthur, 77
Herzl, Theodor, 108f
Hillel, 10
Hitler, 114
Holocaust, 113f
    reactions to, 100
Holy days, 129f
Homeland, Jewish, 122

Immigration Act, 95
Inquisition, 63f
Isaac, Jules, 123
Israel
    physical and spiritual, 43
    state of, 122

Jefferson, Thomas, 96
Jewish context of early
    Christianity, 7
Jewish rebellions, 25
Johanan ben Zakkai, 16, 24
John, evangelist, and Jews, 19
Joselit, Jenna W., 94
Josephus, 46f
Judaism
    branches of, 85ff
    diversity of, 87
    pluralism of, 8
    religio licta, 26
    restoration of, 17
    and temple loss, 16
Justin Martyr, 37, 43, 48

Kabbala, 68
Kaplan, Mordecai, 86
King, Martin L., 102f
Ku Klux Klan, 98f

Law and grace, 13
Legislation, anti-Jewish, 52

Lewis, Bernard, 122
Liebman, Charles S., 87
Life style of early Judaism, 8
Luther, Martin, 73

Maccabees, 9
Maimonides, 58
Marcionism, 38
Margolis, Max L., 52f
Marranos, 66
Martyrology, 45
Marx, Alexander, 52f
Massacres, 59
Mendelssohn, Moses M., 82
Midrash, 33
Minim, 17
Mishnah, 34
Mob rule, 60
Montesquieu, Charles de, 76
Moran, Gabriel, 42
Mussner, Franz, 57
Mysticism, Jewish, 67, 92

National Socialism, history of, 116f
Nativism, 93f
Nazarenes, 18
Neusner, Jacob, 32, 34
Newport, R.I. community, 81
Nicea, Council of, 53
Nihilism, 114f
Noah, as prefiguration, 37
Noahide laws, 132
Nostra Aetate, 124

O'Brien, Conor C., 112

Pagan dogmas, 108
Palestinian Judaism, 6
Parkes, James, 45

Parousia, 13f
Passion plays, 66
Paul, apostle
  letters of, 12
  polemic of, 13
Peoplehood, 87
People's Party, 109
Persecutions, reasons for, 59, 64
Pharisees, 8, 24
Pittsburgh Platform, 83
Pogroms, 78
Poland, Jews in, 65f
Poliakov, Leon, 61
Popes and Jews, 54, 58
Populism, 95
Potok, Chaim, 70
Prayer, 136f
Prejudice, 7

Rabbis, 10
Racial antisemitism, 6
Racism, 94f, 108
Raphael, Marc L., 82
Ritual murder, 60
Roulle, 61
Ruether, Rosemary R., 40, 57, 106

Sabbatai Zevi, 69
Sabbath, 129
  activities on, 35
Sacrifice in Judaism, 132
Sadducees, 8
Salvation, 72
Sanctification of daily life, 35
Sanders, E.P., 43
Sarna, Jonathan D., 92
Sephardim, 66
Sermon on the Mount, 14
Shammai, 11
Shema Israel, 87, 130

Smallwood, E. Mary, 27
Song of Songs, 37
Spinoza, Baruch, 75
Steinberg, Milton, 80
Story, Joseph, 96
Study and prayer, 34
Suffering servant, 37
Synagogue
    expulsion from, 17
    institution, 87, 133
    Jesus' followers and, 17

Talmud, 29, 33, 36
    burning of, 58
    and scriptures, 37
Teaching of contempt, 6
    oral, 33, 37
    written, 39
Temple, 131
    destruction of, 16
Theodosian Code, 53
Theological prejudice, 7
Three-legged chair, 16, 127ff
Tillich, Paul, 118
Tocqueville, Alexis de, 97
Toleration in debasement, 56

Torah
    and gentiles, 11
    meaning of, 127
Tosefta, 34
Touro synagogue, 82
Tzaddikim, 70

Universalism, 75
    of St. Paul, 15
Usury, 61

Vance, Zebulon, 97

Wandering Jew, 65
Washing, ritual, 136, 138
Weinberger, Moses, 84f
Winter, Paul, 44
Wise, Isaac M., 82f
Wisdom literature, 67
World Council of Churches, 123
Worship, 134
Wright, Richard, 101

Yavneh, 16
Yiddish, 65

Zealots, 8
Zionism, history of, 108ff

other volumes in this series

Stepping Stones to Further Jewish-Christian Relations: An Unabridged Collection of Christian Documents, compiled by Helga Croner (A Stimulus Book, 1977).

Helga Croner and Leon Klenicki, editors, *Issues in the Jewish-Christian Dialogue: Jewish Perspectives on Covenant, Mission and Witness* (A Stimulus Book, 1979).

Clemens Thoma, *A Christian Theology of Judaism* (A Stimulus Book, 1980).

Helga Croner, Leon Klenicki and Lawrence Boadt, C.S.P., editors, *Biblical Studies: Meeting Ground of Jews and Christians* (A Stimulus Book, 1980).

John T. Pawlikowski, O.S.M., *Christ in the Light of the Christian-Jewish Dialogue* (A Stimulus Book, 1982).

Martin Cohen and Helga Croner, editors, *Christian Mission-Jewish Mission* (A Stimulus Book, 1982).

Leon Klenicki and Gabe Huck, editors, *Spirituality and Prayer: Jewish and Christian Understandings* (A Stimulus Book, 1983).

Leon Klenicki and Geoffrey Wigoder, editors, *A Dictionary of the Jewish-Christian Dialogue* (A Stimulus Book, 1984).

Edward Flannery, *The Anguish of the Jews* (A Stimulus Book, 1985).

More Stepping Stones to Jewish-Christian Relations: An Unabridged Collection of Christian Documents 1975–1983, compiled by Helga Croner (A Stimulus Book, 1985).

Clemens Thoma and Michael Wyschogrod, editors, *Understanding Scripture: Explorations of Jewish and Christian Traditions of Interpretation* (A Stimulus Book, 1987).

Bernard J. Lee, S.M., *The Galilean Jewishness of Jesus* (A Stimulus Book, 1988).

Clemens Thoma and Michael Wyschogrod, editors, *Parable and Story in Judaism and Christianity* (A Stimulus Book, 1989).

Eugene J. Fisher and Leon Klenicki, editors, *In Our Time: The Flowering of Jewish–Catholic Dialogue* (A Stimulus Book, 1990).

Leon Klenicki, editor, *Toward a Theological Encounter* (A Stimulus Book, 1991).

David Burrell and Yehezkel Landau, editors, *Voices from Jerusalem* (A Stimulus Book, 1991).

STIMULUS BOOKS are developed by Stimulus Foundation, a not-for-profit organization, and are published by Paulist Press. The Foundation wishes to further the publication of scholarly books on Jewish and Christian topics that are of importance to Judaism and Christianity.

Stimulus Foundation was established by an erstwhile refugee from Nazi Germany who intends to contribute with these publications to the improvement of communication between Jews and Christians.

Books for publication in this Series will be selected by a committee of the Foundation, and offers of manuscripts and works in progress should be addressed to:

Stimulus Foundation
785 West End Ave.
New York, N.Y. 10025